Charles D. Provan

The Church Is Israel Now

The Transfer of Conditional Privilege

D1569641

ROSS
HOUSE
BOOKS

Vallecito, California

Ross House Books
PO Box 67, Vallecito, CA 95251
www.rosshousebooks.org

Library of Congress Control Number: 2003094473
ISBN: 1-879998-39-4

Printed in the United States of America

The Church
Is Israel Now

Neither circumcision nor uncircumcision means anything; what counts is a new creation. Peace and mercy to all who follow this rule, even to the Israel of God.

Galatians 6:15-16

OLD AND NEW TESTAMENT SCRIPTURE TEXTS
WHICH ILLUSTRATE
THE CONDITIONAL PRIVILEGED POSITION
AND TITLES
OF "RACIAL ISRAEL"
AND THEIR TRANSFER TO THE CHRISTIAN CHURCH

ARRANGED WITH COMMENTS
BY THE AUTHOR

THE CHURCH IS ISRAEL NOW

This booklet is one of the end products of several years of research into the topic of Old Testament prophecy and its relationship to the New Testament. When I first attempted to understand these things, I thought I would use the quotes of the Old Testament found in the New Testament and try to let the Apostles show me how to interpret the Old Testament. I was soon puzzled by the occurrences I found, for Old Testament passages which referred to Israel kept popping up in the New Testament referring to the Christians. How was this possible? How did the Apostles (over and over again) apply "Israel passages" to Christians?

Moving into related areas, such as the titles of the Church and titles of Israel, I found that the same terms used in the Old Testament to describe Israel are used in the New Testament to describe Christians. The only hypothesis which explains how this could be is that the Israel of the Old Testament (so-called "Racial Israel") had been replaced by the Israel of the New Testament, the Christian Church. The privileges and responsibilities of "Racial Israel" now belong to believers in Christ. A verse which demonstrates the transition quite clearly is Matthew 21:43, which reads, "Therefore I tell you that the kingdom of God will be taken away from you and given to a people who will produce its fruit." Here, Jesus states that "the kingdom of God", which Israel actually had in Old Testament times, was (shortly before crucifixion) transferred to anyone (regardless of race, etc.) who did the will of God.

From that time on, the Old Testament passages which had hitherto applied to the much-blessed but continually disobedient nation of Israel, now applied to the followers of Christ. In the process of transfer, however, the Old Testament was stripped of (formerly legitimate) ideas such as circumcision, geographical limits on worship, temples made of stone and wood, and racial nationalism.

As you examine the passages contained in this booklet, hopefully you will come to realize some of the marvelous blessings to which Christians (of Jewish or Gentile descent) are entitled (with responsibilities, of course!). The Christian Church will be seen as the New Israel of God, not as some unplanned activities of God while he awaits the long-delayed return to him of "Racial Israel"!

This booklet will seek to prove, using Old and New Testament Scriptures, that:

1) "Racial Israelites" who disobey God are, by the teachings of the Old and New Testaments, deposed from whatever blessings they may formerly have been entitled to by racial descent. In other words, those who are Jews by race only are not Jews at all in the eyes of God.

2) The Christian Church (and we do not mean any particular denomination of Christians by this term) is now the Israel of God, according to the teachings of the New Testament. The Church is seen to be Israel by the following facts:

a) the Old Testament titles of Israel are the New Testament titles of the Christian Church, and;

b) Old Testament passages which clearly and indisputably refer to Israel are quoted by the Apostles of Christ as referring to the Christian Church.

As for "2a", we may here humorously remind our readers that if someone sees a bird that looks, quacks, waddles, and feels like a duck and in the New Testament is called a duck — then the creature so described is, indeed, a duck! As for "2b", if the Apostles say that so-and-so Old Testament passage about Israel is about the Church, we may logically deduce that the Church of Christ is the real Israel now, and has taken "Racial Israel's" place — or else the Apostles were wrong (quite often!). As the second option is repugnant to Christians, then the first remains: the Church is Israel now.

Charles D. Provan

Monongahela, Pa.
September 21, 1987

TABLE OF CONTENTS

THIS LISTING CONTAINS THE BOLD-TYPED VERSES OF
THE BOOK IN THE ORDER OF THEIR APPEARANCE

SECTION 1

OLD TESTAMENT TITLES AND ATTRIBUTES OF
ISRAEL WHICH ARE, IN THE NEW TESTAMENT,
REFERRED TO THE CHRISTIAN CHURCH

SECTION 2

OLD TESTAMENT VERSES REFERRING TO ISRAEL WHICH ARE QUOTED IN THE NEW TESTAMENT AS REFERRING TO THE CHRISTIANS

SECTION 3

OLD TESTAMENT ETHICAL COMMANDS TO ISRAEL WHICH ARE QUOTED IN THE NEW TESTAMENT AS APPLYING TO THE CHURCH

SECTION 1

Old Testament Titles And Attributes Of Israel Which Are, In The New Testament, Referred To The Christian Church

Titles and attributes are in bold type so that the reader may notice them more easily. The surrounding (non-bold) verses are included so that the context may be examined.

These Scripture passages demonstrate that the Christian Church is Israel now because of the fact that the Old Testament titles and attributes of Israel are applied en masse to the Church in the New Testament.

Where available, we have also included various Old and New Testament scriptures which **deny** these same titles and attributes to **disobedient** Israel.

THE BELOVED OF GOD

A. Israel Is Beloved Of God

Exodus 15:13-16
[13]"**In your unfailing love** you will lead the people you have redeemed. In your strength you will guide them to your holy dwelling. [14]The nations will hear and tremble; anguish will grip the people of Philistia. [15]The chiefs of Edom will be terrified, the leaders of Moab will be seized with trembling, the people of Canaan will melt away; [16]terror and dread will fall upon them. By the power of your arm they will be as still as a stone — until your people pass by, O Lord, until the people you bought pass by."

Deuteronomy 33:1-4
[1]This is the blessing that Moses the man of God pronounced on the Israelites before his death. [2]He said: "The Lord came from Sinai and dawned over them from Seir; he shone forth from Mount Paran. He came with myriads of holy ones from the south, from his mountain slopes. [3]**Surely it is you who love the people**; all the holy ones are in your hand. At your feet they all bow down, and from you receive instruction, [4]the law that Moses gave us, the possession of the assembly of Jacob."

Ezra 3:10-11
[10]When the builders laid the foundation of the temple of the Lord, the priests in their vestments and with trumpets, and the Levites (the sons of Asaph) with cymbals, took their places to praise the Lord, as prescribed by David king of Israel. [11]With praise and thanksgiving they sang to the Lord:"He is good; **his love to Israel endures forever.**" And all the people gave a great shout of praise to the Lord, because the foundation of the house of the Lord was laid.

****

Some may be confused by the use of the word "forever" in this passage, and may come to the conclusion that God's love for Israel is unconditional. However, this is clearly not the case, unless we say that Scripture contradicts itself, for, in the following section, we will examine Scripture which states that God hates Israel when Israel is in a state of disobedience. To further illustrate the Scripture's interpretation of the word "forever", please refer to 1 Samuel 2:30 (page 21), where the same word is used.

****

B. Disobedient Israel Is Not Beloved Of God

Leviticus 26:27-30
[27]"If in spite of this you still do not listen to me but continue to be hostile toward me, [28]then **in my anger I will be hostile toward you**, and I myself

will punish you for your sins seven times over. ²⁹You will eat the flesh of your sons and the flesh of your daughters. ³⁰I will destroy your high places, cut down your incense altars and pile your dead bodies on the lifeless forms of your idols, and **I will abhor you."**

Jeremiah 12:8
⁸My inheritance has become to me like a lion in the forest. She roars at me; therefore **I hate her.**

Jeremiah 16:5-7
⁵For this is what the Lord says: "Do not enter a house where there is a funeral meal; do not go to mourn or show sympathy, because **I have withdrawn my blessing, my love and my pity from this people,"** declares the Lord. ⁶"Both high and low will die in this land. They will not be buried or mourned, and no one will cut himself or shave his head for them. ⁷No one will offer food to comfort those who mourn for the dead--not even for a father or a mother--nor will anyone give them a drink to console them."

Hosea 9:10-15
¹⁰"When I found Israel, it was like finding grapes in the desert; when I saw your fathers, it was like seeing the early fruit on the fig tree. But when they came to Baal Peor, they consecrated themselves to that shameful idol and became as vile as the thing they loved. ¹¹Ephraim's glory will fly away like a bird--no birth, no pregnancy, no conception. ¹²Even if they rear children, I will bereave them of every one. Woe to them when I turn away from them! ¹³I have seen Ephraim, like Tyre, planted in a pleasant place. But Ephraim will bring out their children to the slayer." ¹⁴Give them, O Lord--what will you give them? Give them wombs that miscarry and breasts that are dry. ¹⁵"Because of all their wickedness in Gilgal, **I hated them there.** Because of their sinful deeds, I will drive them out of my house. **I will no longer love them;** all their leaders are rebellious."

Amos 9:7-8
⁷"**Are not you Israelites the same to me as the Cushites?**" declares the Lord. "Did I not bring Israel up from Egypt, the Philistines from Caphtor and the Arameans from Kir? ⁸Surely the eyes of the Sovereign Lord are on the sinful kingdom. I will destroy it from the face of the earth--yet I will not totally destroy the house of Jacob," declares the Lord.

Matthew 3:7
⁷But when he saw many of the Pharisees and Sadducees coming to where he was baptizing, he said to them: "**You brood of vipers!** Who warned you to flee from the coming wrath?"

Philippians 3:2
²Watch out for **those dogs, those men who do evil, those mutilators of the flesh.**

4

1 Thessalonians 2:14-16
[14]"For you, brothers, became imitators of God's churches in Judea, which are in Christ Jesus; You suffered from your own countrymen the same things those churches suffered from **the Jews** [15]**who killed the Lord Jesus and the prophets and also drove us out. They displease God and are hostile to all men** [16]**in their effort to keep us from speaking to the Gentiles so that they may be saved. In this way they always heap up their sins to the limit. The wrath of God has come upon them at last.**

Titus 1:10-11
[10]"For there are **many rebellious people, mere talkers and deceivers, especially those of the circumcision group.** [11]"They must be silenced, because they are ruining whole households by teaching things they ought not to teach--and that for the sake of dishonest gain.

C. The Christians Are Beloved Of God

Romans 9:22-25
[22]"What if God, choosing to show his wrath and make his power known, bore with great patience the objects of his wrath--prepared for destruction? [23]"What if he did this to make the riches of his glory known to the objects of his mercy, whom he prepared in advance for glory-- [24]"even us, whom he also called, not only from the Jews but also from the Gentiles? [25]"As he says in Hosea: "I will call them 'my people' who are not my people; and **I will call her 'my loved one' who is not my loved one.**"

Ephesians 5:1-2
[1]"Be imitators of God, therefore, as **dearly beloved children** [2]"and live a life of love, just as Christ loved us and gave himself up for us as a fragrant offering and sacrifice to God.

Colossians 3:5-12
[5]"Put to death, therefore, whatever belongs to your earthly nature: sexual immorality, impurity, lust, evil desires and greed, which is idolatry. [6]"Because of these, the wrath of God is coming. [7]"You used to walk in these ways, in the life you once lived. [8]"But now you must rid yourselves of all such things as these: anger, rage, malice, slander, and filthy language from your lips. [9]"Do not lie to each other, since you have taken off your old self with its practices [10]"and have put on the new self, which is being renewed in knowledge in the image of its Creator. [11]"Here there is no Greek or Jew, circumcised or uncircumcised, barbarian, Scythian, slave or free, but Christ is all, and is in all. [12]"Therefore, **as God's chosen people, holy and dearly loved**, clothe yourselves with compassion, kindness, humility, gentleness and patience.

1 John 3:1
[1]"**How great is the love the Father has lavished on us**, that we should be called children of God! And that is what we are! The reason the world does not know us is that it did not know him.

THE CHILDREN OF GOD

A. Israelites Are The Children Of God

Exodus 4:21-23
²¹The Lord said to Moses, "When you return to Egypt, see that you perform before Pharaoh all the wonders I have given you the power to do. But I will harden his heart so that he will not let the people go. ²²Then say to Pharaoh, 'This is what the Lord says: **Israel is my firstborn son,** ²³and I told you, "Let my son go, so he may worship me." But you refused to let him go; so I will kill your firstborn son.' "

Deuteronomy 14:1-2
¹**You are the children of the Lord your God.** Do not cut yourselves or shave the front of your heads for the dead, ²for you are a people holy to the Lord your God. Out of all the peoples on the face of the earth, the Lord has chosen you to be his treasured possession.

Isaiah 1:1-4
¹The vision concerning Judah and Jerusalem that Isaiah son of Amoz saw during the reigns of Uzziah, Jotham, Ahaz and Hezekiah, kings of Judah. ²Hear, O heavens! Listen, O earth! For the Lord has spoken: "**I reared children and brought them up, but they have rebelled against me.** ³The ox knows his master, the donkey his owner's manger, but Israel does not know, my people do not understand." ⁴Ah, sinful nation, a people loaded with guilt, a brood of evildoers, **children given to corruption!** They have forsaken the Lord; they have spurned the Holy One of Israel and turned their backs on him.

Isaiah 63:7-10
⁷I will tell of the kindnesses of the Lord, the deeds for which he is to be praised, according to all the Lord has done for us--yes, the many good things he has done for the house of Israel, according to his compassion and many kindnesses. ⁸He said, "Surely they are my people, **sons** who will not be false to me"; and so he became their Savior. ⁹In all their distress he too was distressed, and the angel of his presence saved them. In his love and mercy he redeemed them; he lifted them up and carried them all the days of old. ¹⁰Yet they rebelled and grieved his Holy Spirit. So he turned and became their enemy and he himself fought against them.

Jeremiah 31:7-10
⁷This is what the Lord says: "Sing with joy for Jacob; shout for the foremost of the nations. Make your praises heard, and say, 'O Lord, save your people, the remnant of Israel.' ⁸See, I will bring them from the land of the north and gather them from the ends of the earth. Among them will be the blind and the lame, expectant mothers and women in labor; a great throng will return. ⁹They will come with weeping; they will pray as I bring them back. I will lead them beside streams of water on a level path where they will not stumble, because **I am Israel's father, and Ephraim is my firstborn son.** ¹⁰"Hear

the word of the Lord, O nations; proclaim it in distant coastlands; 'He who scattered Israel will gather them and will watch over his flock like a shepherd.

Hosea 11:1-2
[1]"When Israel was a child, I loved him, and **out of Egypt I called my son.** [2]But the more I called Israel, the further they went from me. They sacrificed to the Baals and they burned incense to images.

B. Disobedient Israelites Are Not The Children Of God

Deuteronomy 32:5
[5]They have acted corruptly toward him; to their shame **they are no longer his children,** but a warped and crooked generation.

John 8:37-44
[37]I know you are Abraham's descendants. Yet you are ready to kill me, because you have no room for my word. [38]I am telling you what I have seen in the Father's presence, and you do what you have heard from your father." [39]"**Abraham is our father,**" they answered. "**If you were Abraham's children,**" said Jesus, "**then you would do the things Abraham did.** [40]As it is, you are determined to kill me, a man who has told you the truth that I heard from God. Abraham did not do such things. [41]You are doing the things your own father does." "We are not illegitimate children," they protested. "The only father we have is God himself." [42]Jesus said to them, "**If God were your Father, you would love me,** for I came from God and now am here. I have not come on my own; but he sent me. [43]Why is my language not clear to you? Because you are unable to hear what I say. [44]**You belong to your father, the devil,** and you want to carry out your father's desire. He was a murderer from the beginning, not holding to the truth, for there is no truth in him. When he lies, he speaks his native language, for he is a liar and the father of lies.

****

Moses states in Deuteronomy 32:5 that Israelites who "act corruptly toward" God are "no longer his [God's] children." And Jesus says that Israelites who do evil things are in reality children of the Devil, not of God.

****

C. The Christians Are The Children Of God

John 1:11-13
¹¹He came to that which was his own, but his own did not receive him. ¹²Yet to all who received him, **to those who believed in his name, he gave the right to become children of God**-- ¹³children born not of natural descent, nor of human decision or a husband's will, but born of God.

John 11:49-52
⁴⁹Then one of them, named Caiaphas, who was high priest that year, spoke up, "You know nothing at all! ⁵⁰You do not realize that it is better for you that one man die for the people than that the whole nation perish." ⁵¹He did not say this on his own, but as high priest that year he prophesied that Jesus would die for the Jewish nation, ⁵²**and not only for that nation but also for the scattered children of God**, to bring them together and make them one.

Romans 8:13-16
¹³For if you live according to the sinful nature, you will die; but if by the Spirit you put to death the misdeeds of the body, you will live, ¹⁴because **those who are led by the Spirit of God are sons of God.** ¹⁵For you did not receive a spirit that makes you a slave again to fear, but you received the Spirit of sonship. And by him we cry, "Abba, Father." ¹⁶The Spirit himself testifies with our spirit that **we are God's children.**

2 Corinthians 6:14-18
¹⁴Do not be yoked together with unbelievers. For what do righteousness and wickedness have in common? Or what fellowship can light have with darkness? ¹⁵What harmony is there between Christ and Belial? What does a believer have in common with an unbeliever? ¹⁶What agreement is there between the temple of God and idols? For we are the temple of the living God. As God has said: "I will live with them and walk among them, and I will be their God, and they will be my people." ¹⁷"Therefore come out from them and be separate, says the Lord. Touch no unclean thing, and I will receive you." ¹⁸**"I will be a Father to you, and you will be my sons and daughters, says the Lord Almighty."**

Galatians 3:26-28
²⁶**You are all sons of God through faith in Christ Jesus,** ²⁷for all of you who were baptized into Christ have clothed yourselves with Christ. ²⁸There is neither Jew nor Greek, slave nor free, male nor female, for you are all one in Christ Jesus.

Galatians 4:4-7
⁴But when the time had fully come, God sent his Son, born of a woman, born under the law, ⁵to redeem those under the law, **that we might receive the full rights of sons.** ⁶Because **you are sons,** God sent the Spirit of his Son into our hearts, the Spirit who calls out, "Abba, Father." ⁷So you are no longer a slave, **but a son; and since you are a son,** God has made you also an heir.

Philippians 2:14-16

[14]Do everything without complaining or arguing, [15]so that you may become blameless and pure, **children of God** without fault in a crooked and depraved generation, in which you shine like stars in the universe [16]as you hold out the word of life--in order that I may boast on the day of Christ that I did not run or labor for nothing.

1 John 3:1

[1]How great is the love the Father has lavished on us, **that we should be called children of God!** And that is what we are! The reason the world does not know us is that it did not know him.

THE FIELD OF GOD

A. Israel Is The Field Of God

Jeremiah 12:7-12

[7]"I will forsake my house, abandon my inheritance; I will give the one I love into the hands of her enemies. [8]My inheritance has become to me like a lion in the forest. She roars at me; therefore I hate her. [9]Has not my inheritance become to me like a speckled bird of prey that other birds of prey surround and attack? Go and gather all the wild beasts; bring them to devour. [10]Many shepherds will ruin my vineyard and trample down **my field**; they will turn my pleasant field into a desolate wasteland. [11]It will be made a wasteland, parched and desolate before me; the whole land will be laid waste because there is no one who cares. [12]Over all the barren heights in the desert destroyers will swarm, for the sword of the Lord will devour from one end of the land to the other; no one will be safe.

B. The Christians Are The Field Of God

1 Corinthians 3:5-9

[5]What, after all, is Apollos? And what is Paul? Only servants, through whom you came to believe--as the Lord has assigned to each his task. [6]I planted the seed, Apollos watered it, but God made it grow. [7]So neither he who plants nor he who waters is anything, but only God, who makes things grow. [8]The man who plants and the man who waters have one purpose, and each will be rewarded according to his own labor. [9]For we are God's fellow workers; **you are God's field**, God's Building.

THE FLOCK OF GOD AND OF THE MESSIAH

A. Israel Is The Flock Of God And Of The Messiah

Psalm 78:52-55
⁵²But he brought his people out **like a flock; he led them like sheep** through the desert. ⁵³He guided them safely, so they were unafraid; but the sea engulfed their enemies. ⁵⁴Thus he brought them to the border of his holy land, to the hill country his right hand had taken. ⁵⁵He drove out nations before them and allotted their lands to them as an inheritance; he settled the tribes of Israel in their homes.

Psalm 80:1-3
¹**Hear us, O Shepherd of Israel, you who lead Joseph like a flock**; you who sit enthroned between the cherubim, shine forth ²before Ephraim, Benjamin and Manasseh. Awaken your might; come and save us. ³Restore us, O God; make your face shine upon us, that we may be saved.

Isaiah 40:9-11
⁹You who bring good tidings to Zion, go up on a high mountain. You who bring good tidings to Jerusalem, lift up your voice with a shout, lift it up, do not be afraid; say to the towns of Judah, "Here is your God!" ¹⁰See, the Sovereign Lord comes with power, and his arm rules for him. See, his reward is with him, and his recompense accompanies him. ¹¹**He tends his flock like a shepherd; He gathers the lambs in his arms and carries them close to his heart**; he gently leads those that have young.

Jeremiah 23:1-3
¹"Woe to the shepherds who are destroying and scattering **the sheep of my pasture!**" declares the Lord. ²Therefore this is what the Lord, the God of Israel, says to the shepherds who tend my people: "Because you have scattered **my flock** and driven them away and have not bestowed care on them, I will bestow punishment on you for the evil you have done," declares the Lord. ³"I myself will gather the remnant of **my flock** out of all the countries where I have driven them and will bring them back to their pasture, where they will be fruitful and increase in number.

Jeremiah 31:10-12
¹⁰"Hear the word of the Lord, O nations; proclaim it in distant coastlands: **'He who scattered Israel will gather them and will watch over his flock like a shepherd.'** ¹¹For the Lord will ransom Jacob and redeem them from the hand of those stronger than they. ¹²They will come and shout for joy on the heights of Zion; they will rejoice in the bounty of the Lord--the grain, the new wine and the oil, the young of the flocks and herds. They will be like a well-watered garden, and they will sorrow no more.

Ezekiel 34:12-16
¹²**As a shepherd looks after his scattered flock when he is with them, so will I look after my sheep.** I will rescue them from all the places where

they were scattered on a day of clouds and darkness. ¹³I will bring them out from the nations and gather them from the countries, and I will bring them into their own land. I will pasture them on the mountains of Israel, in the ravines and in all the settlements in the land. ¹⁴I will tend them in a good pasture, and the mountain heights of Israel will be their grazing land. There they will lie down in good grazing land, and there they will feed in a rich pasture on the mountains of Israel. ¹⁵**I myself will tend my sheep** and have them lie down, declares the Sovereign Lord. ¹⁶I will search for the lost and bring back the strays. I will bind up the injured and strengthen the weak, but the sleek and the strong I will destroy. **I will shepherd the flock** with justice.

Micah 5:2-4
²"But you, Bethlehem Ephrathah, though you are small among the clans of Judah, out of you will come for me one who will be ruler over Israel, whose origins are from of old, from ancient times." ³Therefore Israel will be abandoned until the time when she who is in labor gives birth and the rest of his brothers return to join the Israelites. ⁴**He will stand and shepherd his flock in the strength of the Lord**, in the majesty of the name of the Lord his God. And they will live securely, for then his greatness will reach to the ends of the earth.

****

This passage refers to the nation of Israel as the flock of the Messianic King, that is, the Christ. (Here it is worth pointing out that the term "Messiah" is Hebrew for "Anointed One". The common designation "Christ" is just the Greek equivalent of "Messiah", as both "Christ" and "Messiah" mean the same thing.)

****

Zechariah 10:3-5
³"My anger burns against the shepherds, and I will punish the leaders; for the Lord God Almighty will care for **his flock, the house of Judah**, and make them like a proud horse in battle. ⁴From Judah will come the cornerstone, from him the tent peg, from him the battle bow, from him every ruler. ⁵Together they will be like mighty men trampling the muddy streets in battle. Because the Lord is with them, they will fight and overthrow the horsemen.

B. The Christians Are The Flock Of God And Of The Messiah

John 10:14-16
¹⁴"**I am the good shepherd**; I know my sheep and my sheep know me--¹⁵just as the Father knows me and I know the Father--and I lay down my life for the sheep. ¹⁶**I have other sheep that are not of this sheep pen. I must bring them also. They too will listen to my voice, and there shall be one flock and one shepherd.**

Hebrews 13:20-21

²⁰May the God of peace, who through the blood of the eternal covenant brought back from the dead **our Lord Jesus, that great Shepherd of the sheep,** ²¹equip you with everything good for doing his will, and may he work in us what is pleasing to him, through Jesus Christ, to whom be glory for ever and ever. Amen.

1 Peter 2:25

²⁵For you were **like sheep** going astray, but now you have returned to the **Shepherd and Overseer of your souls.**

1 Peter 5:1-3

¹To the elders among you, I appeal as a fellow elder, a witness of Christ's sufferings and one who also will share in the glory to be revealed: ²**Be shepherds of God's flock that is under your care,** serving as overseers-- not because you must, but because you are willing, as God wants you to be; not greedy for money, but eager to serve; ³not lording it over those entrusted to you, but being examples to **the flock.**

THE HOUSE OF GOD

A. Israel Is The House Of God

Numbers 12:1-9
¹Miriam and Aaron began to talk against Moses because of his Cushite wife, for he had married a Cushite. ²"Has the Lord spoken only through Moses?" they asked. "Hasn't he also spoken through us?" And the Lord heard this. ³(Now Moses was a very humble man, more humble than anyone else on the face of the earth.) ⁴At once the Lord said to Moses, Aaron and Miriam, "Come out to the Tent of Meeting, all three of you." So the three of them came out. ⁵Then the Lord came down in a pillar of cloud; he stood at the entrance to the Tent and summoned Aaron and Miriam. When both of them stepped forward, ⁶he said, "Listen to my words: "When a prophet of the Lord is among you, I reveal myself to him in visions, I speak to him in dreams. ⁷But this is not true of my servant Moses; **he is faithful in all my house.** ⁸With him I speak face to face, clearly and not in riddles; he sees the form of the Lord. Why then were you not afraid to speak against my servant Moses?" ⁹The anger of the Lord burned against them, and he left them.

B. The Christians Are The House Of God

1 Timothy 3:15
¹⁵if I am delayed, you will know how people ought to conduct themselves in **God's household, which is the church of the living God,** the pillar and foundation of the truth.

Hebrews 3:1-6
¹Therefore, holy brothers, who share in the heavenly calling, fix your thoughts on Jesus, the apostle and high priest whom we confess. ²He was faithful to the one who appointed him, just as **Moses was faithful in all God's house.** ³Jesus has been found worthy of greater honor than Moses, just as the builder of a house has greater honor than the house itself. ⁴For every house is built by someone, but God is the builder of everything. ⁵**Moses was faithful as a servant in all God's house,** testifying to what would be said in the future. ⁶ But Christ is faithful as a son over **God's house. And we are his house, if we hold on to our courage and the hope of which we boast.**

Hebrews 10:21-22
²¹and since **we have a great priest over the house of God,** ²²let us draw near to God with a sincere heart in full assurance of faith, having our hearts sprinkled to cleanse us from a guilty conscience and having our bodies washed with pure water.

1 Peter 4:17
¹⁷For it is time for judgment to begin with **the family [Greek: house] of God; and if it begins with us,** what will the outcome be for those who do not obey the gospel of God?

THE KINGDOM OF GOD

A. Israel Is The Kingdom Of God

Exodus 19:1-6

¹In the third month after the Israelites left Egypt--on the very day--they came to the Desert of Sinai. ²After they set out from Rephidim, they entered the Desert of Sinai, and Israel camped there in the desert in front of the mountain. ³Then Moses went up to God, and the Lord called to him from the mountain and said, "This is what you are to say to the house of Jacob and what you are to tell the people of Israel: ⁴"You yourselves have seen what I did to Egypt, and how I carried you on eagles' wings and brought you to myself. ⁵Now if you obey me fully and keep my covenant, then out of all nations you will be my treasured possession. Although the whole earth is mine, **⁶you will be for me a kingdom of priests and a holy nation.'** These are the words you are to speak to the Israelites."

1 Chronicles 17:7-14

⁷"Now then, tell my servant David, 'This is what the Lord Almighty says: I took you from the pasture and from following the flock, to be ruler over my people Israel. ⁸I have been with you wherever you have gone, and I have cut off all your enemies from before you. Now I will make your name like the names of the greatest men of the earth. ⁹And I will provide a place for my people Israel and will plant them so that they can have a home of their own and no longer be disturbed. Wicked people will not oppress them anymore, as they did at the beginning ¹⁰and have done ever since the time I appointed leaders over my people Israel. I will also subdue all your enemies.

"'I declare to you that the Lord will build a house for you: ¹¹When your days are over and you go to be with your fathers, I will raise up your offspring to succeed you, one of your own sons, and I will establish his kingdom. ¹²He is the one who will build a house for me, and I will establish his throne forever. ¹³I will be his father, and he will be my son. I will never take my love away from him, as I took it away from your predecessor. ¹⁴I will set him over my house and **my kingdom** forever; his throne will be established forever.'"

1 Chronicles 28:2-7

²King David rose to his feet and said: "Listen to me, my brothers and my people. I had it in my heart to build a house as a place of rest for the ark of the covenant of the Lord, for the footstool of our God, and I made plans to build it. ³But God said to me, 'You are not to build a house for my Name, because you are a warrior and have shed blood.' ⁴"Yet the Lord, the God of Israel, chose me from my whole family to be king over Israel forever. He chose Judah as leader, and from the house of Judah he chose my family, and from my father's sons he was pleased to make me king over all Israel. ⁵Of all my sons--and the Lord has given me many--**he has chosen my son Solomon to sit on the throne of the kingdom of the Lord over Israel.** ⁶He said to me: 'Solomon your son is the one who will build my house and my courts, for I have chosen him to be my son, and I will be his father. ⁷I will establish his kingdom forever if he is unswerving in carrying out my commands and laws, as is being done at this time.'

15

B. Disobedient Israel Is Not The Kingdom Of God

Matthew 8:10-12

[10]When Jesus heard this, he was astonished and said to those following him, "I tell you the truth, I have not found anyone in Israel with such great faith. [11]I say to you that many will come from the east and the west, and will take their places at the feast with Abraham, Isaac and Jacob in **the kingdom of heaven.** [12]**But the subjects of the kingdom will be thrown outside,** into the darkness, where there will be weeping and gnashing of teeth."

Matthew 21:43, 45

[43]"Therefore I tell you that **the kingdom of God will be taken away from you and given to a people who will produce its fruit....** [45]When the chief priests and the Pharisees heard Jesus' parables, they knew he was talking about them.

C. The Christians Are The Kingdom Of God

Romans 14:17-19

[17]For **the kingdom of God** is not a matter of eating and drinking, but of righteousness, peace and joy in the Holy Spirit, [18]because anyone who serves Christ in this way is pleasing to God and approved by men. [19]Let us therefore make every effort to do what leads to peace and to mutual edification.

1 Corinthians 4:18-21

[18]Some of you have become arrogant, as if I were not coming to you. [19]But I will come to you very soon, if the Lord is willing, and then I will find out not only how these arrogant people are talking, but what power they have. [20]For **the kingdom of God** is not a matter of talk but of power. [21]What do you prefer? Shall I come to you with a whip, or in love and with a gentle spirit?

Colossians 1:10-14

[10]And we pray this in order that you may live a life worthy of the Lord and may please him in every way: bearing fruit in every good work, growing in the knowledge of God, [11]being strengthened with all the power according to his glorious might so that you may have great endurance and patience, and joyfully [12]giving thanks to the Father, who has qualified you to share in the inheritance of the saints in the kingdom of light. [13]For he has rescued us from the dominion of darkness and **brought us into the kingdom of the Son he loves,** [14]in whom we have redemption, the forgiveness of sins.

Colossians 4:10-11

[10]My fellow prisoner Aristarchus sends you his greetings, as does Mark, the cousin of Barnabas. (You have received instructions about him; if he comes to you, welcome him.) [11]Jesus, who is called Justus, also sends greetings. These are the only Jews among **my fellow workers for the kingdom of God,** and they have proved a comfort to me.

Revelation 1:4-6

⁴John,

To the seven churches in the province of Asia:

Grace and peace to you from him who is, and who was, and who is to come, and from the seven spirits before his throne, ⁵and from Jesus Christ, who is the faithful witness, the firstborn from the dead, and the ruler of the kings of the earth. To him who loves us and has freed us from our sins by his blood, ⁶and **has made us to be a kingdom** and priests to serve his God and Father--to him be the glory and the power forever and ever! Amen.

THE PEOPLE OF GOD

A. The Israelites Are The People Of God

Exodus 6:6-7

⁶"Therefore, say to the Israelites: 'I am the Lord, and I will bring you out from under the yoke of the Egyptians. I will free you from being slaves to them, and I will redeem you with an outstretched arm and with mighty acts of judgment. ⁷**I will take you as my own people**, and I will be your God. Then you will know that I am the Lord your God, who brought you out from under the yoke of the Egyptians.'"

Deuteronomy 27:9

⁹Then Moses and the priests, who are Levites, said to all Israel, "Be silent, O Israel, and listen! **You have now become the people of the Lord your God.**

2 Samuel 7:23

²³And who is like **your people Israel–the one nation on earth that God went out to redeem as a people for himself,** and to make a name for himself, and to perform great and awesome wonders by driving out nations and their gods from before your people, whom you redeemed from Egypt?

Jeremiah 11:2-4

²"Listen to the terms of this covenant and tell them to the people of Judah and to those who live in Jerusalem, ³Tell them that this is what the Lord, the God of Israel, says: 'Cursed is the man who does not obey the terms of this covenant–ʹthe terms I commanded your forefathers when I brought them out of Egypt, out of the iron-smelting furnace.' I said, 'Obey me and do everything I command you, and **you will be my people, and I will be your God.**

B. Disobedient Israelites Are Not The People Of God

Hosea 1:8-10

⁸After she had weaned Lo-Ruhamah, Gomer had another son. ⁹Then the Lord said, "Call him Lo-Ammi, for **you are not my people,** and I am not your God. ¹⁰"Yet the Israelites will be like the sand on the seashore, which cannot be measured or counted. In the place where it was said to them, 'You are not my people,' they will be called 'sons of the living God.'

Jeremiah 5:10-11

¹⁰"Go through her vineyards and ravage them, but do not destroy them completely. Strip off her branches, for **these people do not belong to the Lord.** ¹¹The house of Israel and the house of Judah have been utterly unfaithful to me," declares the Lord.

Though many people have the impression that the Jews are the people of God, yet these verses from the Old Testament demonstrate that if a Jew does what is evil in the sight of the Lord, he is not a member of the people of God.

C. The Christians Are The People Of God

Romans 9:22-26

²²What if God, choosing to show his wrath and make his power known, bore with great patience the objects of his wrath--prepared for destruction? ²³What if he did this to make the riches of his glory known to the objects of his mercy, whom he prepared in advance for glory-- ²⁴even us, whom he also called, not only from the Jews but also from the Gentiles? ²⁵As he says in Hosea: "**I will call them 'my people' who are not my people;** and I will call her 'my loved one' who is not my loved one," ²⁶and, "It will happen that in the very place where it was said to them, 'You are not my people,' they will be called 'sons of the living God.'"

2 Corinthians 6:14-16

¹⁴Do not be yoked together with unbelievers. For what do righteousness and wickedness have in common? Or what fellowship can light have with darkness? ¹⁵What harmony is there between Christ and Belial? What does a believer have in common with an unbeliever? ¹⁶What agreement is there between the temple of God and idols? For we are the temple of the living God. As God has said: "I will live with them and walk among them, and I will be their God, and **they will be my people.**"

Ephesians 4:11-13

¹¹It was he who gave some to be apostles, some to be prophets, some to be evangelists, and some to be pastors and teachers, ¹²to prepare **God's people** for works of service, so that the body of Christ may be built up ¹³until we all reach unity in the faith and in the knowledge of the Son of God and become mature, attaining to the whole measure of the fullness of Christ.

Ephesians 5:1-3

¹Be imitators of God, therefore, as dearly loved children ²and live a life of love, just as Christ loved us and gave himself up for us as a fragrant offering and sacrifice to God. ³But among you there must not be even a hint of sexual immorality, or of any kind of impurity, or of greed, because these are improper for **God's holy people.**

2 Thessalonians 1:9-10

⁹They will be punished with everlasting destruction and shut out from the presence of the Lord and from the majesty of his power ¹⁰on the day he comes to be glorified in **his holy people** and to be marveled at among all those who have believed. **This includes you,** because you believed our testimony to you.

Titus 2:11-14

[11]For the grace of God that brings salvation has appeared to all men. [12]It teaches us to say "No" to ungodliness and worldly passions, and to live self-controlled, upright godly lives in this present age, [13]while we wait for the blessed hope--the glorious appearing of our great God and Savior, Jesus Christ, [14]who gave himself for us to redeem us from all wickedness and to purify for himself **a people that are his very own**, eager to do what is good.

THE PRIESTS OF GOD

A. The Israelites Are The Priests Of God

Exodus 19:1-6
[1]In the third month after the Israelites left Egypt--on the very day--they came to the Desert of Sinai. [2]After they set out from Rephidim, they entered the Desert of Sinai, and Israel camped there in the desert in front of the mountain. [3]Then Moses went up to God, and the Lord called to him from the mountain and said, "This is what you are to say to the house of Jacob and what you are to tell the people of Israel: [4]"You yourselves have seen what I did to Egypt, and how I carried you on eagles' wings and brought you to myself. [5]Now if you obey me fully and keep my covenant, then out of all nations you will be my treasured possession. Although the whole earth is mine, [6]**you will be for me a kingdom of priests** and a holy nation.' These are the words you are to speak to the Israelites."

B. Disobedient Israelites Are Not The Priests Of God

1 Samuel 2:27-34
[27]Now a man of God came to Eli and said to him, "This is what the Lord says: 'Did I not clearly reveal myself to your father's house when they were in Egypt under Pharoah? [28]I chose your father out of all the tribes of Israel **to be my priest**, to go up to my altar, to burn incense, and to wear an ephod in my presence. I also gave your father's house all the offerings made with fire by the Israelites. [29]Why do you scorn my sacrifice and offering that I prescribed for my dwelling? Why do you honor your sons more than me by fattening yourselves on the choice parts of every offering made by my people Israel?'
[30]"Therefore the Lord, the God of Israel, declares: '**I promised that your house and your father's house would minister before me forever.**' But now the Lord declares: '**Far be it from me! Those who honor me I will honor, but those who despise me will be disdained.** [31]The time is coming when I will cut short your strength and the strength of your father's house, so that there will not be an old man in your family line [32]and you will see distress in my dwelling. Although good will be done to Israel, in your family line there will never be an old man. [33]Every one of you that I do not cut off from my altar will be spared only to blind your eyes with tears and to grieve your heart, and all your descendants will die in the prime of life.
[34]"'And what happens to your two sons, Hophni and Phinehas, will be a sign to you--they will both die on the same day.

Lamentations 4:13-16
[13]But it happened because of the sins of her prophets and **the iniquities of her priests**, who shed within her the blood of the righteous. [14]Now they grope through the streets like men who are blind. They are so defiled with blood that no one dares to touch their garments. [15]"Go away! You are unclean!" men cry to them. "Away! Away! Don't touch us!" When they

flee and wander about, people among nations say, "They can stay here no longer." [16]The Lord himself has scattered them; he no longer watches over them. **The priests are shown no honor,** the elders no favor.

Ezekiel 44:10-13
[10]**"The Levites who went far from me** when Israel went astray and who wandered from me after their idols must bear the consequences of their sin. [11]They may serve in my sanctuary, having charge of the gates of the temple and serving in it; they may slaughter the burnt offerings and sacrifices for the people and stand before the people and serve them. [12]But because they served them in the presence of their idols and made the house of Israel fall into sin, therefore I have sworn with uplifted hand that they must bear the consequences of their sin, declares the Sovereign Lord. [13]**They are not to come near to serve me as priests** or come near any of my holy things or my most holy offerings; they must bear the shame of their detestable practices.

Hosea 4:6
[6]my people are destroyed from lack of knowledge. "Because you have rejected knowledge, **I also reject you as my priests;** because you have ignored the law of your God, I also will ignore your children.

****

Some people think that if God says that someone is a priest, he is always a priest. This view is seen to be incorrect. Sin results in the person's disqualification from the priesthood. When Eli's family sinned, they were excluded from the priesthood (1 Samuel 2:30). When the priests of Ezekiel's time "went astray", they ceased to be priests (Ezekiel 44:13). When the nation of Israel rejected the knowledge of God, God rejected Israel as his priests (Hosea 4:6). This would dispose of the view that Israel had, or has, an unconditional covenant with God for the priesthood.

****

Malachi 2:1-9
[1]"And now this admonition is for you, O priests. [2]If you do not listen, and if you do not set your heart to honor my name," says the Lord Almighty, "I will send a curse upon you, and I will curse your blessings. **Yes, I have already cursed them, because you have not set your heart to honor me.** [3]"Because of you I will rebuke your descendants; I will spread on your faces the offal from your festival sacrifices, and you will be carried off with it. [4]And you will know that I have sent you this admonition **so that my covenant with Levi may continue,"** says the Lord Almighty. [5]"My covenant was with him, a covenant of life and peace, and I gave them to him; this called for reverence and he revered me and stood in awe of my name. [6]True instruction was in his mouth and nothing false was found on his lips. He walked with me in peace and uprightness, and turned many from sin. [7]"For the lips of a priest ought to preserve knowledge, and from his mouth men should seek instruction-- because he is the messenger of the Lord Almighty. [8]But you have turned from the way and by your teaching have caused many to

stumble; **you have violated the covenant with Levi,"** says the Lord Almighty. **⁹"So I have caused you to be despised and humiliated before all the people, because you have not followed my ways but have shown partiality in matters of the law."**

****
Note that the message of Malachi to the priests of Israel is that they must repent, or God will discontinue his "covenant with Levi." Since the Levitical priesthood hasn't existed for the past 1900 years, which is longer than it existed (c. 1600 years), it evidently was cancelled by God due to the sins of the people and priests of Israel.
****

C. The Christians Are The Priests Of God

1 Peter 2:4-10
⁴As you come to him, the living stone--rejected by men but chosen by God and precious to him-- **⁵you also, like living stones, are being built into a spiritual house to be a holy priesthood,** offering spiritual sacrifices acceptable to God through Jesus Christ. ⁶For in Scripture it says: "See, I lay a stone in Zion, a chosen and precious cornerstone, and the one who trusts in him will never be put to shame." ⁷Now to you who believe, this stone is precious. But to those who do not believe, "The stone the builders rejected has become the capstone," ⁸and, "A stone that causes men to stumble and a rock that makes them fall." They stumble because they disobey the message--which is also what they were destined for. ⁹But you are a chosen people, **a royal priesthood,** a holy nation, a people belonging to God, that you may declare the praises of him who called you out of the darkness into his wonderful light. ¹⁰Once you were not a people, but now you are the people of God; once you had not received mercy, but now you have received mercy.

Revelation 1:4-6
⁴John, To the seven churches in the province of Asia: Grace and peace to you from him who is, and who was, and who is to come, and from the seven spirits before his throne, ⁵and from Jesus Christ, who is the faithful witness, the firstborn from the dead, and the ruler of the kings of the earth. To him who loves us and has freed us from our sins by his blood, ⁶and **has made us to be a kingdom and priests** to serve his God and Father--to him be glory and power for ever and ever! Amen.

Revelation 5:9-10
⁹And they sang a new song: "You are worthy to take the scroll and to open its seals, because you were slain, and with your blood you purchased men for God from every tribe and language and people and nation. ¹⁰**You have made them to be a kingdom and priests** to serve our God, and they will reign on the earth."

THE VINEYARD OF GOD

A. Israel Is The Vineyard Of God

Isaiah 5:1-7

[1]I will sing for the one I love a song about his vineyard: My loved one had a vineyard on a fertile hillside. [2]He dug it up and cleared it of stones and planted it with choicest vines. He built a watchtower in it and cut out a winepress as well. Then he looked for a crop of good grapes, but it yielded only bad fruit. [3]"Now you dwellers in Jerusalem and men of Judah, judge between me and **my vineyard**. [4]What more could have been done for **my vineyard** than I have done for it? When I looked for good grapes, why did it yield only bad? [5]Now I will tell you what I am going to do to **my vineyard**: I will take away its hedge, and it will be destroyed; I will break down its wall, and it will be trampled. [6]I will make it a wasteland, neither pruned nor cultivated, and briers and thorns will grow there. I will command the clouds not to rain on it." [7]**The vineyard of the Lord Almighty is the house of Israel**, and the men of Judah are the garden of his delight. And he looked for justice, but saw bloodshed; for righteousness, but heard cries of distress.

Jeremiah 12:7-12

[7]"I will forsake my house, abandon my inheritance; I will give the one I love into the hands of her enemies. [8]My inheritance has become to me like a lion in the forest. She roars at me; therefore I hate her. [9]Has not my inheritance become to me like a speckled bird of prey that other birds of prey surround and attack? Go and gather all the wild beasts; bring them to devour. [10]Many shepherds will ruin **my vineyard** and trample down my field; they will turn my pleasant field into a desolate wasteland. [11]It will be made a wasteland, parched and desolate before me; the whole land will be laid waste because there is no one who cares. [12]Over all the barren heights in the desert destroyers will swarm, for the sword of the Lord will devour from one end of the land to the other; no one will be safe.

B. The Christians Are The Vineyard Of God

Luke 20:9-16

[9]He went on to tell the people this parable: "A man planted a vineyard, rented it to some farmers and went away for a long time. [10]At harvest time he sent a servant to the tenants so they would give him some of the fruit of the vineyard. But the tenants beat him and sent him away empty-handed. [11]He sent another servant, but that one also they beat and treated shamefully and sent away empty-handed. [12]He sent still a third, and they wounded him and threw him out. [13]"Then the owner of the vineyard said, 'What shall I do? I will send my son, whom I love; perhaps they will respect him.' [14]"But when the tenants saw him, they talked the matter over. 'This is the heir,' they said. 'Let's kill him, and the inheritance will be ours.' [15]So they threw him out of the vineyard and killed him. "What then will the owner of the

vineyard do to them? ¹⁶He will come and kill those tenants and **give the vineyard to others**." When the people heard this, they said, "May this never be!"

****

Jesus here tells the people of Israel that when "the son of the vineyard owner" (Jesus) is killed by the "the tenants" (the Jews), that "the owner of the vineyard" (God) will "give the vineyard to others" (that is, the righteous among the Gentiles). This does not prove that the Jews cannot be part of the vineyard. It means that the vineyard ("Israelite status") is now given without regard to racial descent.

****

THE WIFE (OR BRIDE) OF GOD

A. Israel Is The Wife (Or Bride) Of God

Isaiah 54:4-7
4"'Do no be afraid; you will not suffer shame. Do not fear disgrace; you will not be humiliated. You will forget the shame of your youth and remember no more the reproach of your widowhood. **5For your Maker is your husband-- the Lord Almighty is his name**--the Holy One of Israel is your Redeemer; he is called God of all the earth. **6**The Lord will call you back as if you were a **wife** deserted and distressed in spirit--**a wife** who married young, only to be rejected," says your God. 7"'For a brief moment I abandoned you, but with deep compassion I will bring you back.

Jeremiah 2:2-3
2"Go and proclaim in the hearing of Jerusalem: "'I remember the devotion of your youth, how **as a bride you loved me** and followed me through the desert, through a land not sown. 3Israel was holy to the Lord, the firstfruits of his harvest; all who devoured her were held guilty, and disaster overtook them,'" declares the Lord.

Ezekiel 16:1-3, 32
1The word of the Lord came to me: 2"'Son of man, confront Jerusalem with her detestable practices 3and say, 'This is what the Sovereign Lord says to Jerusalem: Your ancestry and birth were in the land of the Canaanites; your father was an Amorite and your mother a Hittite.... 32"'**You adulterous wife!** You prefer strangers to your own husband!

Hosea 1:2-6
2When the Lord began to speak through Hosea, the Lord said to him, "**Go, take to yourself an adulterous wife and children of unfaithfulness, because the land is guilty of the vilest adultery in departing from the Lord.**" 3So he married Gomer daughter of Diblaim, and she conceived and bore him a son. 4Then the Lord said to Hosea, "Call him Jezreel, because I will soon punish the house of Jehu for the massacre at Jezreel, and I will put an end to the kingdom of Israel. 5In that day I will break Israel's bow in the Valley of Jezreel." 6Gomer conceived again and gave birth to a daughter. Then the Lord said to Hosea, "Call her Lo-Ruhamah, for I will no longer show love to the house of Israel, that I should at all forgive them.

B. Disobedient Israel Is Not The Wife (Or Bride) Of God

Jeremiah 3:6-8
6During the reign of King Josiah, the Lord said to me, "Have you seen what faithless Israel has done? She has gone up on every high hill and under every spreading tree and has committed adultery there. 7I thought that after she had done all this she would return to me but she did not, and her unfaithful

26

sister Judah saw it. **⁸I gave faithless Israel her certificate of divorce and sent her away because of all her adulteries.** Yet I saw that her unfaithful sister Judah had no fear; she also went out and committed adultery.

Hosea 2:2-3
²"Rebuke your mother, rebuke her, for **she is not my wife, and I am not her husband.** Let her remove the adulterous look from her face and the unfaithfulness from between her breasts. ³Otherwise I will strip her naked and make her as bare as on the day she was born; I will make her like a desert, turn her into a parched land, and slay her with thirst.

C. The Christians Are The Wife (Or Bride) Of God

2 Corinthians 11:2-3
²I am jealous for you with a godly jealousy. **I promised you to one husband, to Christ,** so that I might present you as a pure virgin to him. ³But I am afraid that just as Eve was deceived by the serpent's cunning, your minds may somehow be led astray from your sincere and pure devotion to Christ.

Ephesians 5:25-32
²⁵Husbands, love your wives, just as Christ loved the church and gave himself up for her ²⁶to make her holy, cleansing her by the washing with water through the word, ²⁷and to present her to himself as a radiant church, without stain or wrinkle or any other blemish, but holy and blameless. ²⁸In this same way, husbands ought to love their wives as their own bodies. He who loves his wife loves himself. ²⁹After all, no one ever hated his own body, but he feeds and cares for it, just as Christ does the church-- ³⁰for we are members of his body. ³¹**"For this reason a man will leave his father and mother and be united to his wife, and the two will become one flesh."** ³²**This is a profound mystery--but I am talking about Christ and the church.**

****

Much is made of the fact that Israel "is the bride of God himself." What is not referred to is the Biblical fact that if Israel is in a state of sin (such as rejecting the Christ) they are divorced from God. The Church is now the wife of Christ (who is, as we know from the Old and the New Testaments, God).

****

THE CHILDREN OF ABRAHAM

A. The Israelites Are The Children Of Abraham

2 Chronicles 20:7-9
[7]O our God, did you not drive out the inhabitants of this land before your people Israel and give it forever to **the descendants of Abraham your friend**? [8]They have lived in it and have built in it a sanctuary for your Name, saying, [9]"If calamity comes upon us, whether the sword of judgment, or plague or famine, we will stand in your presence before this temple that bears your Name and will cry out to you in our distress, and you will hear us and save us.'

Psalm 105:4-6
[4]Look to the Lord and his strength; seek his face always. [5]Remember the wonders he has done, his miracles, and the judgments he pronounced, [6]**O descendants of Abraham his servant**, O sons of Jacob, his chosen ones.

Isaiah 41:8-16
[8]"But you, O Israel, my servant Jacob, whom I have chosen, **you descendants of Abraham my friend**, [9]I took you from the ends of the earth, from its farthest corners I called you. I said, 'You are my servant'; I have chosen you and have not rejected you. [10]So do not fear, for I am with you; do not be dismayed, for I am your God. I will strengthen you and help you; I will uphold you with my righteous right hand. [11]"All who rage against you will surely be ashamed and disgraced; those who oppose you will be as nothing and perish. [12]Though you search for your enemies, you will not find them. Those who wage war against you will be as nothing at all. [13]For I am the Lord, your God, who takes hold of your right hand and says to you, Do not fear; I will help you. [14]Do not be afraid, O worm Jacob, O little Israel, for I myself will help you," declares the Lord, your Redeemer, the Holy One of Israel. [15]"See, I will make you into a threshing sledge, new and sharp, with many teeth. You will thresh the mountains and crush them, and reduce the hills to chaff. [16]You will winnow them, the wind will pick them up, and a gale will blow them away. But you will rejoice in the Lord and glory in the Holy One of Israel.

B. Disobedient Israelites Are Not The Children Of Abraham

John 8:37-44
[37]I know you are Abraham's descendants. Yet you are ready to kill me, because you have no room for my word. [38]I am telling you what I have seen in the father's presence, and you do what you have heard from your Father." [39]**"Abraham is our father,"** they answered. **"If you were Abraham's children,"** said Jesus, **"then you would do the things Abraham did.** [40]As it is, you are determined to kill me, a man who has told you the truth that I heard from God. Abraham did not do such things. [41]You are doing the

things your own father does." "We are not illegitimate children," they protested. "The only Father we have is God himself." ⁴²Jesus said to them, "If God were your Father, you would love me, for I came from God and now am here. I have not come on my own; but he sent me. ⁴³Why is my language not clear to you? Because you are unable to hear what I say. ⁴⁴You belong to your father, the devil, and you want to carry out your father's desire. He was a murderer from the beginning, not holding to the truth, for there is no truth in him. When he lies, he speaks his native language, for he is a liar and the father of lies.

****

Jesus in this passage agrees that the people he is talking with were physically descendants of Abraham. Yet in the eyes of God this counted for nothing if they desired to kill Jesus, "a man who told the truth he heard from God." On the contrary, to be regarded as the true sons of Abraham, one must "do the things Abraham did."

****

Romans 9:6-7
⁶It is not as though God's word had failed. For **not all who are descended from Israel are Israel.** ⁷**Nor because they are his descendants are they all Abraham's children.** On the contrary, "It is through Isaac that your offspring will be reckoned."

****

Most people think of the Jews as the children of Abraham. Yet Scripture records that Abraham had many other children besides Isaac, through whom the Jews trace their lineage (a fact which is greatly open to dispute). In Genesis 16:16, Abraham had a son by Hagar, and in Genesis 25:1-2, Abraham is said to have had six more sons by Keturah, another wife of his. Yet God stated to Abraham that the descendants of Abraham would be reckoned through Isaac, the child born to Abraham through faith in God. Paul says that this fact demonstrates that the true children of Abraham are reckoned as those who have the faith of Abraham, not those who can trace mere physical descent from Abraham.

****

Galatians 4:21-31
²¹Tell me, you who want to be under the law, are you not aware of what the law says? ²²For it is written that Abraham had two sons, one by the slave woman and the other by the free woman. ²³His son by the slave woman was born in the ordinary way; but his son by the free woman was born as the result of a promise. ²⁴These things may be taken figuratively, for the women represent two covenants. One covenant is from Mount Sinai and bears children who are to be slaves: This is Hagar. ²⁵**Now Hagar stands for Mount Sinai in Arabia and corresponds to the present city of Jerusalem, because she is in slavery with her children.** ²⁶But the

Jerusalem that is above is free, and she is our mother. [27]For it is written: "Be glad, O barren woman, who bears no children; break forth and cry aloud, you who have no labor pains; because more are the children of the desolate woman than of her who has a husband." [28]Now you, brothers, like Isaac, are children of promise. [29]At that time the son born in the ordinary way persecuted the son born by the power of the Spirit. It is the same now. [30]But what does the Scripture say? **"Get rid of the slave woman and her son, for the slave woman's son will never share in the inheritance with the free woman's son."** [31]Therefore, brothers, we are not children of the slave woman, but of the free woman.

****

Paul, quoting God in Genesis, says that those who are merely Jews by racial descent have no share in the inheritance of the true sons of Abraham, that is, the Christians.

****

C. The Christians Are The Children Of Abraham

Romans 4:9-16
[9]Is this blessedness only for the circumcised, or also for the uncircumcised? We have been saying that Abraham's faith was credited to him as righteousness. [10]Under what circumstances was it credited? Was it after he was circumcised, or before? It was not after, but before! [11]And he received the sign of circumcision, a seal of the righteousness that he had by faith while he was still uncircumcised. **So then, he is the father of all who believe but have not been circumcised**, in order that righteousness might be credited to them. [12]And he is also the father of the circumcised who not only are circumcised but who also walk in the footsteps of the faith that our father Abraham had before he was circumcised. [13]It was not through law that Abraham and his offspring received the promise that he would be heir of the world, but through the righteousness that comes by faith. [14]For if those who live by law are heirs, faith has no value and the promise is worthless, [15]because law brings wrath. And where there is no law there is no transgression. [16]Therefore, the promise comes by faith, so that it may be by grace and may be guaranteed to **all Abraham's offspring**--not only to those who are of the law but **also to those who are of the faith of Abraham. He is the father of us all.**

Galatians 3:6-9
[6]Consider Abraham: "He believed God, and it was credited to him as righteousness." [7]Understand, then, that **those who believe are children of Abraham**. [8]The Scripture foresaw that God would justify the Gentiles by faith, and announced the gospel in advance to Abraham: "All nations will be blessed through you." [9]So those who have faith are blessed along with Abraham, the man of faith.

Galatians 3:26-29

[26]You are all sons of God through faith in Christ Jesus, [27]for all of you who were baptized into Christ have clothed yourselves with Christ. [28]There is neither Jew nor Greek, slave nor free, male nor female, for you are all one in Christ Jesus. [29]**If you belong to Christ, then you are Abraham's seed,** and heirs according to the promise.

Galatians 4:21-31

[21]Tell me, you who want to be under the law, are you not aware of what the law says? [22]For it is written that Abraham had two sons, one by the slave woman and the other by the free woman. [23]His son by the slave woman was born in the ordinary way; but **his son by the free woman was born as the result of a promise.** [24]These things may be taken figuratively, for the women represent two covenants. One covenant is from Mount Sinai and bears children who are to be slaves: This is Hagar. [25]Now Hagar stands for Mount Sinai in Arabia and corresponds to the present city of Jerusalem, because she is in slavery with her children. [26]But the Jerusalem that is above is free, and she is our mother. [27]For it is written: "Be glad, O barren woman, who bears no children; break forth and cry aloud, you who have no labor pains; because more are the children of the desolate woman than of her who has a husband." [28]**Now you, brothers, like Isaac, are children of promise.** [29]At that time the son born in the ordinary way persecuted the son born by the power of the Spirit. It is the same now. [30]But what does the Scripture say? "Get rid of the slave woman and her son, for the slave woman's son will never share in the inheritance with the free woman's son." [31]**Therefore, brothers, we are not children of the slave woman, but of the free woman.**

****

We can see from these verses that the true sons of Abraham are those who have the faith of Abraham, those who belong to Christ.

****

THE CHOSEN PEOPLE

A. The Israelites Are The Chosen People

Deuteronomy 7:7-8
[7]The Lord did not set his affection on you and **choose you** because you were more numerous than other peoples, for you were the fewest of all peoples. [8]But it was because the Lord loved you and kept the oath he swore to your forefathers that he brought you out with a mighty hand and redeemed you from the land of slavery, from the power of Pharoah king of Egypt.

Deuteronomy 10:14-15
[14]To the Lord your God belong the heavens, even the highest heavens, the earth and everything in it. [15]Yet the Lord set his affection on your forefathers and loved them, and **he chose you, their descendants**, above all the nations, as it is today.

Deuteronomy 14:1-2
[1]You are the children of the Lord your God. Do not cut yourselves or shave the front of your heads for the dead, [2]for you are a people holy to the Lord your God. Out of all the peoples on the face of the earth, **the Lord has chosen you to be his treasured possession.**

Isaiah 43:18-24
[18]"Forget the former things; do not dwell on the past. [19]See, I am doing a new thing! Now it springs up; do you not perceive it? I am making a way in the desert and streams in the wasteland. [20]The wild animals honor me, the jackals and the owls, because I provide water in the desert and streams in the wasteland, to give drink to my people, **my chosen, [21]the people I formed for myself that they may proclaim my praise.** [22]"Yet you have not called upon me, O Jacob, you have not wearied yourselves for me, O Israel. [23]You have not brought me sheep for burnt offerings, nor honored me with your sacrifices. I have not burdened you with grain offerings nor wearied you with demands for incense. [24]You have not bought any fragrant calamus for me, or lavished on me the fat of your sacrifices. But you have burdened me with your sins and wearied me with your offenses.

B. Disobedient Israelites Are Not The Chosen People

Deuteronomy 31:16-18
[16]And the Lord said to Moses: "You are going to rest with your fathers, and these people will soon prostitute themselves to the foreign gods of the land they are entering. They will forsake me and break the covenant I made with them. [17]On that day I will become angry with them **and forsake them;** I will hide my face from them, and they will be destroyed. Many disasters and difficulties will come upon them, and on that day they will ask, 'Have not these disasters come upon us because our God is not with us? [18]And I will certainly hide my face on that day because of all their wickedness in turning to other gods.

2 Kings 17:13-20

[13]The Lord warned Israel and Judah through all his prophets and seers: "Turn from your evil ways. Observe my commands and decrees, in accordance with the entire Law that I commanded your fathers to obey and that I delivered to you through my servants the prophets." [14]But they would not listen and were as stiff-necked as their fathers, who did not trust in the Lord their God. [15]They rejected his decrees and the covenant he had made with their fathers and the warnings he had given them. They followed worthless idols and themselves became worthless. They imitated the nations around them although the Lord had ordered them, "Do not do as they do," and they did the things the Lord had forbidden them to do. [16]They forsook all the commands of the Lord their God and made for themselves two idols cast in the shape of calves, and an Asherah pole. They bowed down to all the starry hosts, and they worshiped Baal. [17]They sacrificed their sons and daughters in the fire. They practiced divination and sorcery and sold themselves to do evil in the eyes of the Lord, provoking him to anger. [18]So the Lord was very angry with Israel and removed them from his presence. Only the tribe of Judah was left, [19]and even Judah did not keep the commands of the Lord their God. They followed the practices Israel had introduced. [20]Therefore, **the Lord rejected all the people of Israel**; he afflicted them and gave them into the hands of plunderers, until he thrust them from his presence.

2 Chronicles 25:5-7

[5]Amaziah called the people of Judah together and assigned them according to their families to commanders of thousands and commanders of hundreds for all Judah and Benjamin. He then mustered those twenty years old or more and found that there were three hundred thousand men ready for military service, able to handle the spear and shield. [6]He also hired a hundred thousand fighting men from Israel for a hundred talents of silver. [7]But a man of God came to him and said, "O king, these troops from Israel must not march with you, for **the Lord is not with Israel--not with any of the people of Ephraim.**

Psalm 78:58-60

[58]They angered him with their high places; they aroused his jealousy with their idols. [59]When God heard them, he was very angry; **he rejected Israel completely.** [60]He abandoned the tabernacle of Shiloh, the tent he had set up among men.

Jeremiah 6:30

[30]They are called rejected silver, **because the Lord has rejected them.**"

Jeremiah 7:29

[29]Cut off your hair and throw it away; take up a lament on the barren heights, for **the Lord has rejected and abandoned this generation that is under his wrath.**

Jeremiah 14:10

[10]This is what the Lord says about this people: "They greatly love to wander; they do not restrain their feet. **So the Lord does not accept them**; he will now remember their wickedness and punish them for their sins."

C. The Christians Are The Chosen People

Colossians 3:11-16
[11]Here there is no Greek or Jew, circumcised or uncircumcised, barbarian, Scythian, slave or free, but Christ is all, and is in all. [12]Therefore, **as God's chosen people,** holy and dearly loved, clothe yourselves with compassion, kindness, humility, gentleness and patience. [13]Bear with each other and forgive whatever grievances you may have against one another. Forgive as the Lord forgave you. [14]And over all these virtues put on love, which binds them all together in perfect unity. [15]Let the peace of Christ rule in your hearts, since as members of one holy body you were called to peace. And be thankful. [16]Let the word of Christ dwell in you richly as you teach and admonish one another with all wisdom, and as you sing psalms, hymns and spiritual songs with gratitude in your hearts to God.

1 Peter 2:9-10
[9]But **you are a chosen people,** a royal priesthood, a holy nation, a people belonging to God, that you may declare the praises of him who called you out of darkness into his wonderful light. [10]Once you were not a people, but now you are the people of God; once you had not received mercy, but now you have received mercy.

****

Sadly, if people today would be asked, "According to the Bible, who are the chosen people?", we suspect that most would answer: "The Jews, of course!" By this, they would mean those persons who are racially Jews, or those who are followers of Judaism. This shows the sorry state of affairs which exists when the Bible is not studied, because the Bible states that the Christians are the chosen people, chosen not because of racial descent or following the traditions of the Rabbis, but because of faith in and obedience to God.

****

34

THE CIRCUMCISED

A. The Israelites Are The Circumcised

Genesis 17:9-14
[9]Then God said to Abraham, "As for you, you must keep my covenant, you and your descendants after you for the generations to come. [10]This is my covenant with you and your descendants after you, the covenant you are to keep: **Every male among you shall be circumcised.** [11]You are to undergo circumcision, and it will be the sign of the covenant between me and you. [12]For the generations to come every male among you who is eight days old must be circumcised, including those born in your household or bought with money from a foreigner--those who are not your offspring. [13]Whether born in your household or bought with your money, **they must be circumcised.** My covenant in your flesh is to be an everlasting covenant. [14]Any uncircumcised male, who has not been circumcised in the flesh, will be cut off from his people; he has broken my covenant."

Judges 15:14-19
[14]As he approached Lehi, the Philistines came toward him shouting. The Spirit of the Lord came upon him in power. The ropes on his arms became like charred flax, and the bindings dropped from his hands. [15]Finding a fresh jawbone of a donkey, he grabbed it and struck down a thousand men. [16]Then Samson said, "With a donkey's jawbone I have made donkeys of them. With a donkey's jawbone I have killed a thousand men." [17]When he finished speaking, he threw away the jawbone; and the place was called Ramath Lehi. [18]Because he was very thirsty, he cried out to the Lord, "You have given your servant this great victory. Must I now die of thirst and fall into the hands of **the uncircumcised?**" [19]Then God opened up the hollow place in Lehi, and water came out of it. When Samson drank, his strength returned and he revived. So the spring was called En Hakkore, and it is still there in Lehi.

****

Samson calls the Philistines by the name of "the uncircumcised", by which it may be deduced that the Israelites regarded themselves as "the circumcised."

****

B. Disobedient Israelites Are Not The Circumcised

Jeremiah 9:25-26
[25]"The days are coming," declares the Lord, "when I will punish **all who are circumcised only in the flesh**-- [26]Egypt, Judah, Edom, Ammon, Moab and all who live in the desert in distant places. For all these nations are really uncircumcised, and **even the whole house of Israel is uncircumcised in heart.**"

Romans 2:25-29

²⁵Circumcision has value if you observe the law, but **if you break the law, you have become as though you had not been circumcised.** ²⁶If those who are not circumcised keep the law's requirements, will they not be regarded as though they were circumcised? ²⁷The one who is not circumcised physically and yet obeys the law will condemn you who, even though you have the written code and circumcision, are a lawbreaker. ²⁸A man is not a Jew if he is only one outwardly, **nor is circumcision merely outward and physical.** ²⁹No, a man is a Jew if he is one inwardly; and circumcision is circumcision of the heart, by the Spirit, not by the written code. Such a man's praise is not from men, but from God.

Philippians 3:2-3

²Watch out for those dogs, those men who do evil, **those mutilators of the flesh.** ³For it is we who are the circumcision, we who worship by the Spirit of God, who glory in Christ Jesus, and who put no confidence in the flesh.

C. The Christians Are The Circumcised

Romans 2:28-29

²⁸A man is not a Jew if he is only one outwardly, nor is circumcision merely outward and physical. ²⁹No, a man is a Jew if he is one inwardly; and **circumcision is circumcision of the heart, by the Spirit, not by the written code. Such a man's praise is not from men, but from God.**

Philippians 3:2-3

²Watch out for those dogs, those men who do evil, those mutilators of the flesh. ³**For it is we who are the circumcision**, we who worship by the Spirit of God, who glory in Christ Jesus, and who put no confidence in the flesh.

Colossians 2:9-14

⁹For in Christ all the fullness of the Deity lives in bodily form, ¹⁰and you have been given fullness in Christ, who is the head over every power and authority. ¹¹**In him you were also circumcised, in the putting off of the sinful nature, not with a circumcision done by the hands of men but with the circumcision done by Christ,** ¹²having been buried with him in baptism and raised with him through your faith in the power of God, who raised him from the dead. ¹³When you were dead in your sins and in the uncircumcision of your sinful nature, God made you alive with Christ. He forgave us all our sins, ¹⁴having canceled the written code, with its regulations, that was against us and that stood opposed to us; he took it away, nailing it to the cross.

ISRAEL

A. Israel Is Israel

****

As it is obvious that in the Old Testament Israel is Israel, we have not included any Scripture in this first section.

****

B. Disobedient Israelites Are Not Israelites

Numbers 15:30-31
[30]" 'But **anyone who sins defiantly,** whether native-born or alien, blasphemes the Lord, and **that person must be cut off from his people.** [31]Because **he has despised the Lord's word** and broken his commands, **that person must surely be cut off;** his guilt remains on him.' "

****

God here declares that any Israelite who sins defiantly against the word of the Lord must be "cut off from his people." That is, if an Israelite deliberately disobeys the word of God, he is no longer to be regarded as an Israelite, in spite of the fact that some believe in an "unconditional" covenant of God with Israel.

****

Deuteronomy 18:18-19
[18]I will raise up for them a prophet like you from among their brothers; I will put my words in his mouth, and he will tell them everything I command him. [19]If anyone does not listen to **my words** that a prophet speaks in my name, I myself will call him to account.

****

God says in this passage that he is going to send a mighty prophet to Israel, who will arise from among the people of Israel, and will be just like Moses. God himself will tell this prophet what to say to Israel, and when he comes to Israel, the Israelites must obey him or "be called to account," that is, be cut off from membership in Israel. (This is the penalty for disobeying the word of the Lord: Numbers 15:31, above).
Some people say that this passage does not refer to an individual prophet to come, but rather to any prophet at all. This is seen to be incorrect by the fact that right after Moses, Joshua (who was a prophet, Joshua 6:26, 1 Kings 16:34) led Israel, yet Deuteronomy says "Since [Moses' death], no prophet has risen in Israel like Moses...." Therefore, the Deuteronomy passage must refer to an individual great prophet who would arise and lead Israel.

****

Acts 3:20-23

²⁰and that he may send the Christ, who has been appointed for you--even Jesus. ²¹He must remain in heaven until the time comes for God to restore everything, as he promised long ago through his holy prophets. ²²For Moses said, 'The Lord your God will raise up for you a prophet like me from among your own people; you must listen to everything he tells you. ²³**Anyone who does not listen to him will be completely cut off from among his people.'**

****

Peter the Apostle declares to Israel that the prophet who was to come according to Deuteronomy 18:18-19 is none other than Jesus. Further, Peter informs the Jews that any Jew who does not listen to Jesus "will be completely cut off from among his people." This passage explicitly proves that any Jewish person who rejects the words of Jesus is not to be regarded as a member of the nation of Israel.

****

Romans 9:6-7

⁶It is not as though God's word had failed. For **not all who are descended from Israel are Israel.** ⁷Nor because they are his descendants are they all Abraham's children. On the contrary, "It is through Isaac that your offspring will be reckoned."

C. The Christians Are Israel

John 11:49-52

⁴⁹Then one of them, named Caiaphas, who was high priest that year, spoke up, "You know nothing at all! ⁵⁰You do not realize that it is better for you that one man die **for the people** than that **the whole nation** perish." ⁵¹He did not say this on his own, but as high priest that year he prophesied that **Jesus would die for the Jewish nation, ⁵²and not only for that nation but also for the scattered children of God, to bring them together and make them one.**

****

Caiaphas the High Priest prophesied that Jesus would die "for the people [of Israel]". John, interpreting the prophesy, says that this was a prophecy of Christ dying for "the scattered [Gentile] children of God". Therefore, since the crucifixion, both Jewish and Gentile believers in Christ are members of "the people of Israel".

****

1 Corinthians 10:1-4

¹For I do not want you to be ignorant of the fact, **brothers,** that **our forefathers** were all under the cloud and that they all passed through the sea. ²They were all baptized into Moses in the cloud and in the sea. ³They all ate the same spiritual food ⁴and drank the same spiritual drink; for they drank from the spiritual rock that accompanied them, and that rock was Christ.

Paul, talking to Gentile Christians at Corinth, speaks of the Israelites who crossed the Red Sea as "our forefathers"! How is this possible unless the Corinthian Gentile believers in Christ were regarded by Paul as part of the nation of Israel?

Galatians 6:14-16

[14]May I never boast except in the cross of our Lord Jesus Christ, through which the world has been crucified to me, and I to the world. [15]**Neither circumcision nor uncircumcision means anything; what counts is a new creation.** [16]**Peace and mercy to all who follow this rule, even to the Israel of God.**

The real "Israel of God" are those who come to Christ, not those who are merely circumcised.

Ephesians 2:11-22

[11]Therefore, remember that formerly you who are Gentiles by birth and called "uncircumcised" by those who call themselves "the circumcision" (that done in the body by the hands of men)-- [12]remember that **at that time you were separate from Christ, excluded from citizenship in Israel** and foreigners to the covenants of the promise, without hope and without God in the world. [13]But now in Christ Jesus you who once were far away have been brought near through the blood of Christ. [14]For he himself is our peace, who has made the two one and has destroyed the barrier, the dividing wall of hostility, [15]by abolishing in his flesh the law with its commandments and regulations. His purpose was to create in himself one new man out of the two, thus making peace, [16]and in this one body to reconcile both of them to God through the cross, by which he put to death their hostility. [17]He came and preached peace to you who were far away and peace to those who were near. [18]For through him we both have access to the Father by one Spirit. [19]Consequently, **you are no longer foreigners and aliens, but fellow citizens with God's people and members of God's household,** [20]built on the foundation of the apostles and prophets, with Christ Jesus himself as the chief cornerstone. [21]In him the whole building is joined together and rises to become a holy temple in the Lord. [22]And in him you too are being built together to become a dwelling in which God lives by his Spirit.

Paul says that before the Gentile believers came to Christ, they were "excluded from citizenship in Israel". But, through submitting themselves to Christ, these same Gentiles have become "fellow citizens with God's people". Therefore, all people, whether of Jewish or Gentile descent, who come to Christ, are now members of the true nation of Israel.

JERUSALEM

A. Jerusalem Is The City And Mother Of Israel

Psalm 149:2
²Let Israel rejoice in their Maker; let **the people of Zion** be glad in their King.

Isaiah 12:6
⁶Shout aloud and sing for joy, **people of Zion**, for great is the Holy One of Israel among you."

Isaiah 49:14-22
¹⁴But Zion said, "The Lord has forsaken me, the Lord has forgotten me." ¹⁵"Can a mother forget the baby at her breast and have no compassion on the child she has borne? Though she may forget, I will not forget you! ¹⁶See, I have engraved you on the palms of my hands; your walls are ever before me. ¹⁷Your sons hasten back, and those who laid you waste depart from you. ¹⁸Lift up your eyes and look around; **all your sons gather and come to you**. As surely as I live," declares the Lord, "you will wear them all as ornaments; you will put them on, like a bride. ¹⁹"Though you were ruined and made desolate and your land laid waste, now you will be too small for your people, and those who devoured you will be far away. ²⁰**The children born** during your bereavement will yet say in your hearing, 'This place is too small for us; give us some more space to live in.' ²¹Then you will say in your heart, 'Who bore me these? I was bereaved and barren; I was exiled and rejected. Who brought these up? I was left all alone, but these--where have they come from?' " ²²This is what the Sovereign Lord says: "See, I will beckon to the Gentiles, I will lift up my banner to the peoples; **they will bring your sons** in their arms and carry **your daughters** on their shoulders.

Isaiah 51:17-18
¹⁷Awake, awake! Rise up, O Jerusalem, you who have drunk from the hand of the Lord the cup of his wrath, you who have drained to its dregs the goblet that makes men stagger. ¹⁸Of all **the sons she bore** there was none to guide her; of all **the sons she reared** there was none to take her by the hand.

Lamentations 4:2-3
²How **the precious sons of Zion**, once worth their weight in gold, are now considered as pots of clay, the work of a potter's hands! ³Even jackals offer their breasts to nurse their young, but my people have become heartless like ostriches in the desert.

B. Jerusalem Is The City And Mother Of Christians

Galatians 4:21-27
²¹Tell me, you who want to be under the law, are you not aware of what the law says? ²²For it is written that Abraham had two sons, one by the slave

woman and the other by the free woman. ²³His son by the slave woman was born in the ordinary way; but his son by the free woman was born as the result of a promise. ²⁴These things may be taken figuratively, for the women represent two covenants. One covenant is from Mount Sinai and bears children who are to be slaves: This is Hagar. ²⁵Now Hagar stands for Mount Sinai in Arabia and corresponds to the present city of Jerusalem, because she is in slavery with her children. ²⁶But **the Jerusalem that is above is free, and she is our mother.** ²⁷For it is written: "Be glad, O barren woman, who bears no children; break forth and cry aloud, you who have no labor pains; because more are the children of the desolate woman than of her who has a husband."

****

Paul says that Jerusalem is the Mother of the Christians. Therefore, the Christians are the true sons of Zion, as opposed to the sons of Judaistic Zion, who are slaves, according to Paul.

****

Hebrews 12:18-24

¹⁸You have not come to a mountain that can be touched and that is burning with fire; to darkness, gloom and storm; ¹⁹to a trumpet blast or such a voice speaking words that those who heard it begged that no further word be spoken to them, ²⁰because they could not bear what was commanded: "If even an animal touches the mountain, it must be stoned." ²¹The sight was so terrifying that Moses said, "I am trembling with fear." ²²But **you have come to Mount Zion, to the heavenly Jerusalem,** the city of the living God. You have come to thousands upon thousands of angels in joyful assembly, ²³to the church of the firstborn, whose names are written in heaven. You have come to God, the judge of all men, to the spirits of the righteous men made perfect, ²⁴to Jesus the mediator of a new covenant, and to the sprinkled blood that speaks a better word than the blood of Abel.

41

THE JEWS

A. Israelites Are Jews

Ezra 5:1
[1]Now Haggai the prophet and Zechariah the prophet, a descendant of Iddo, prophesied to **the Jews in Judah and Jerusalem** in the name of the God of Israel, who was over them.

Jeremiah 34:8-17
[8]The word came to Jeremiah from the Lord after King Zedekiah had made a covenant with **all the people in Jerusalem** to proclaim freedom for the slaves. [9]Everyone was to free his Hebrew slaves, both male and female; no one was to hold **a fellow Jew** in bondage. [10]So all the officials and people who entered into this covenant agreed that they would free their male and female slaves and no longer hold them in bondage. They agreed, and set them free. [11]But afterward they changed their minds and took back the slaves they had freed and enslaved them again. [12]Then the word of the Lord came to Jeremiah: [13]"This is what the Lord, the God of Israel, says: I made a covenant with your forefathers when I brought them out of Egypt, out of the land of slavery. I said, [14]'Every seventh year each of you must free any fellow Hebrew who has sold himself to you. After he has served you six years, you must let him go free.' Your fathers, however, did not listen to me or pay attention to me. [15]Recently you repented and did what is right in my sight: Each of you proclaimed freedom to his countrymen. You even made a covenant before me in the house that bears my Name. [16]But now you have turned around and profaned my name: each of you has taken back the male and female slaves you had set free to go where they wished. You have forced them to become your slaves again. [17]"Therefore, this is what the Lord says: You have not obeyed me; you have not proclaimed freedom for your fellow countrymen. So I now proclaim 'freedom' for you, declares the Lord--'freedom' to fall by the sword, plague and famine. I will make you abhorrent to all the kingdoms of the earth.

Zechariah 8:18-23
[18]Again the word of the Lord Almighty came to me. [19]This is what the Lord Almighty says: "The fasts of the fourth, fifth, seventh and tenth months will become joyful and glad occasions and happy festivals for Judah. Therefore love truth and peace." [20]This is what the Lord Almighty says: "Many peoples and the inhabitants of many cities will yet come, [21]and the inhabitants of one city will go to another and say, 'Let us go at once to entreat the Lord and seek the Lord Almighty. I myself am going.' [22]And many peoples and powerful nations will come **to Jerusalem** to seek the Lord Almighty and to entreat him." [23]This is what the Lord Almighty says: "In those days ten men from all languages and nations will take firm hold of one **Jew** by the hem of his robe and say, 'Let us go with you, because we have heard that God is with you.' "

B. Disobedient Israelites Are Not Jews

Romans 2:28-29
[28]**A man is not a Jew if he is only one outwardly,** nor is circumcision merely outward and physical. [29]No, a man is a Jew if he is one inwardly; and circumcision is circumcision of the heart, by the Spirit, not by the written code. Such a man's praise is not from men, but from God.

Revelation 2:9
[9]I know your afflictions and your poverty--yet you are rich! I know the slander of **those who say they are Jews and are not, but are a synagogue of Satan.**

Revelation 3:9
[9]I will make those who are **of the synagogue of Satan, who claim to be Jews though they are not, but are liars**--I will make them come and fall down at your feet and acknowledge that I have loved you.

C. Christians Are Jews

Romans 2:28-29
[28]A man is not a Jew if he is only one outwardly, nor is circumcision merely outward and physical. [29]No, **a man is a Jew if he is one inwardly;** and circumcision is circumcision of the heart, by the Spirit, not by the written code. Such a man's praise is not from men, but from God.

THE NEW COVENANT

A. The New Covenant Is With Israel

Jeremiah 31:31-34

[31]"The time is coming," declares the Lord, "when **I will make a new covenant with the house of Israel and with the house of Judah.** [32]It will not be like the covenant I made with their forefathers when I took them by the hand to lead them out of Egypt, because they broke my covenant, though I was a husband to them," declares the Lord. [33]"This is **the covenant I will make with the house of Israel** after that time," declares the Lord. "I will put my law in their minds and write it on their hearts. I will be their God, and they will be my people. [34]No longer will a man teach his neighbor, or a man his brother, saying, 'Know the Lord,' because they will all know me, from the least of them to the greatest," declares the Lord. "For I will forgive their wickedness and will remember their sins no more."

B. The New Covenant Is With Christians

Luke 22:19-20

[19]And he took bread, gave thanks and broke it, and gave it to them, saying, "This is my body given for you; do this in remembrance of me." [20]In the same way, after the supper he took the cup, saying, "This cup is **the new covenant** in my blood, which is poured out for you.

1 Corinthians 11:23-26

[23]For I received from the Lord what I also passed on to you: The Lord Jesus, on the night he was betrayed, took bread, [24]and when he had given thanks, he broke it and said, "This is my body, which is for you; do this in remembrance of me." [25]In the same way, after supper he took the cup, saying, "This cup is **the new covenant** in my blood; do this, whenever you drink it, in remembrance of me." [26]For whenever you eat this bread and drink this cup, you proclaim the Lord's death until he comes.

2 Corinthians 3:4-6

[4]Such confidence as this is ours through Christ before God. [5]Not that we are competent in ourselves to claim anything for ourselves, but our competence comes from God. [6]**He has made us competent as ministers of a new covenant**--not of the letter but of the Spirit; for the letter kills, but the Spirit gives life.

Hebrews 8:6-13

[6]But the ministry Jesus has received is as superior to theirs as **the covenant of which he is mediator is superior to the old one**, and it is founded on better promises. [7]For if there had been nothing wrong with that first covenant, no place would have been sought for another. [8]But God found fault with the people and said: "The time is coming, declares the Lord, when **I will make a new covenant with the house of Israel and with the house of Judah.** [9]It will not be like the covenant I made with their forefathers when I

took them by the hand to lead them out of Egypt, because they did not remain faithful to my covenant, and I turned away from them, declares the Lord. [10]This is **the covenant I will make with the house of Israel** after that time, declares the Lord. I will put my laws in their minds and write them on their hearts. I will be their God, and they will be my people. [11]No longer will a man teach his neighbor, or a man his brother, saying, 'Know the Lord,' because they will all know me, from the least of them to the greatest. [12]For I will forgive their wickedness and will remember their sins no more." [13]By calling this covenant "new", he has made the first one obsolete; and what is obsolete and aging will soon disappear.

AN OLIVE TREE

A. Israel Is An Olive Tree

Jeremiah 11:16-17
[16]**The Lord called you a thriving olive tree** with fruit beautiful in form. But with the roar of a mighty storm he will set it on fire, and its branches will be broken. [17]The Lord Almighty, who planted you, has decreed disaster for you, because the house of Israel and the house of Judah have done evil and provoked me to anger by burning incense to Baal.

Hosea 14:5-6
[5]I will be like the dew to Israel; he will blossom like a lily. Like a cedar of Lebanon he will send down his roots; [6]his young shoots will grow. **His splendor will be like an olive tree,** his fragrance like a cedar of Lebanon.

B. The Christians Are An Olive Tree

Romans 11:17-24
[17]If some of the branches have been broken off, and you, though a wild olive shoot, have been grafted in among the others and now share in the nourishing sap from the olive root, [18]do not boast over those branches. If you do, consider this: You do not support the root, but the root supports you. [19]You will say then, "Branches were broken off so that I could be grafted in." [20]Granted. But they were broken off because of unbelief, and you stand by faith. Do not be arrogant, but be afraid. [21]For if God did not spare the natural branches, he will not spare you either. [22]Consider therefore the kindness and sternness of God; sternness to those who fell, but kindness to you, provided that you continue in his kindness. Otherwise, you also will be cut off. [23]And if they do not persist in unbelief, they will be grafted in, for God is able to graft them in again. [24]After all, if you were cut out of an olive tree that is wild by nature, and contrary to nature were grafted **into a cultivated olive tree,** how much more readily will these, the natural branches, be grafted into **their own olive tree!**

****

The Olive Tree under discussion in Romans 11 is clearly Israel, for it is called "their [Israel's] own olive tree"! Note that Christians of Gentile descent are now part of the tree (Israel), while Jews who have no faith in the Christ have been broken off, as Romans 11:20 says. So, it may be observed that being a true Israelite in the eyes of God depends upon whether one has faith, and is entirely disconnected with a racial background.

****

SECTION 2

Old Testament Verses Referring To Israel
Which Are Quoted In The New Testament
As Referring To The Christians

The quotes themselves are in bold type to call the reader's attention to them. The surrounding (non-bold) verses are included so that the context may be examined.

These verses demonstrate that the New Testament regards the Church as Israel, because of the fact that Old Testament "Israelite" verses are repeatedly quoted as referring to Christians.

QUOTE #1: (Lev. 26:11-12 / Ezek. 37:27 / 2 Cor. 6:16)

Leviticus 26:3-12

[3]"'If you follow my decrees and are careful to obey my commands, [4]I will send you rain in its season, and the ground will yield its crops and the trees of the field their fruit. [5]Your threshing will continue until grape harvest and the grape harvest will continue until planting, and you will eat all the food you want and live in safety in your land. [6]" 'I will grant peace in the land, and you will lie down and no one will make you afraid. I will remove savage beasts from the land, and the sword will not pass through your country. [7]You will pursue your enemies, and they will fall by the sword before you. [8]Five of you will chase a hundred, and a hundred of you will chase ten thousand, and your enemies will fall by the sword before you. [9]" 'I will look on you with favor and make you fruitful and increase your numbers, and I will keep my covenant with you. [10]You will still be eating last year's harvest when you will have to move it out to make room for the new. [11]**I will put my dwelling place among you,** and I will not abhor you. [12]**I will walk among you and be your God, and you will be my people.**

Ezekiel 37:21-28

[21]and say to them, 'This is what the Sovereign Lord says: I will take the Israelites out of the nations where they have gone. I will gather them from all around and bring them back into their own land. [22]I will make them one nation in the land, on the mountains of Israel. There will be one king over all of them and they will never again be two nations or be divided into two kingdoms. [23]They will no longer defile themselves with their idols and vile images or with any of their offenses, for I will save them from all their sinful backsliding, and I will cleanse them. They will be my people, and I will be their God. [24]" 'My servant David will be king over them, and they will all have one shepherd. They will follow my laws and be careful to keep my decrees. [25]They will live in the land I gave to my servant Jacob, the land where your fathers lived. They and their children and their children's children will live there forever, and David my servant will be their prince forever. [26]I will make a covenant of peace with them; it will be an everlasting covenant. I will establish them and increase their numbers, and I will put my sanctuary among them forever. [27]**My dwelling place will be with them; I will be their God, and they will be my people.** [28]Then the nations will know that I the Lord make Israel holy, when my sanctuary is among them forever.'"

2 Corinthians 6:14-16

[14]Do not be yoked together with unbelievers. For what do righteousness and wickedness have in common? Or what fellowship can light have with darkness? [15]What harmony is there between Christ and Belial? What does a believer have in common with an unbeliever? [16]What agreement is there between the temple of God and idols? For we are the temple of the living God. As God has said: **"I will live with them and walk among them, and I will be their God, and they will be my people."**

```
********************************************************************
```
Both the Leviticus and the Ezekiel passages prophesy a time when the Israelites will obey God. God will, in return, bless Israel by making them his people, and by putting his dwelling place among them. In Moses' and Ezekiel's times, this meant that God was going to put a literal temple inside the territory of Israel, and live there. But we see Paul in 2 Corinthians (writing to Gentile Christians who lived in Greece!) applying the prophecies to the Church of Christ. How can this be, unless Paul regards the Christians as the real Israel of God, now under a covenant which has no need for stone and wood temples, or for genealogical restrictions? God does not live in stone buildings any longer, but lives in believers. His blessings are not restricted to the geographical boundaries of a little country in the Middle East, but spread to the whole world! So God fulfills the prophecies of Moses and Ezekiel, but in a non-racial, non-geographical, non-material-building sort of way!

```
********************************************************************
```

QUOTE #2: (Deut. 30:12-14 / Rom. 10:6-8)

Deuteronomy 30:1-14
[1]When all these blessings and curses I have set before you come upon you and you take them to heart wherever the Lord your God disperses you among the nations, [2]and when you and your children return to the Lord your God and obey him with all your heart and with all your soul according to everything I command you today, [3]then the Lord your God will restore your fortunes and have compassion on you and gather you again from all the nations where he scattered you. [4]Even if you have been banished to the most distant land under the heavens, from there the Lord your God will gather you and bring you back. [5]He will bring you to the land that belonged to your fathers, and you will take possession of it. He will make you more prosperous and numerous than your fathers. [6]The Lord your God will circumcise your hearts and the hearts of your descendants, so that you may love him with all your heart and with all your soul, and live. [7]The Lord your God will put all these curses on your enemies who hate and persecute you. [8]You will again obey the Lord and follow all his commands I am giving you today. [9]Then the Lord your God will make you most prosperous in all the work of your hands and in the fruit of your womb, the young of your livestock and the crops of your land. The Lord will again delight in you and make you prosperous, just as he delighted in your fathers, [10]if you obey the Lord your God and keep his commands and decrees that are written in this Book of the Law and turn to the Lord your God with all your heart and with all your soul. [11]Now what I am commanding you today is not too difficult for you or beyond your reach. [12]It is not up to heaven, so that you have to ask, "**Who will ascend into heaven** to get it and proclaim it to us so we may obey it?" [13]Nor is it beyond the sea, so that you have to ask, "**Who will cross the sea** to get it and proclaim it to us so we may obey it?" [14]No, **the word is very near you; it is in your mouth and in your heart** so you may obey it.

50

Romans 10:6-10
⁶But the righteousness that is by faith says: "Do not say in your heart, **'Who will ascend into heaven?'** " (that is, to bring Christ down) ⁷"or **'Who will descend into the deep?'** " (that is, to bring Christ up from the dead). ⁸But what does it say? **"The word is near you; it is in your mouth and in your heart,"** that is, the word of faith we are proclaiming: ⁹That if you confess with your mouth, "Jesus is Lord," and believe in your heart that God raised him from the dead, you will be saved. ¹⁰For it is with your heart that you believe and are justified, and it is with your mouth that you confess and are saved.

****

Paul in Romans takes a passage of Scripture in Deuteronomy which is addressed to Israel and applies it to the Christians. (Some may wonder at the interpretation Paul puts upon the Deuteronomy passage, but upon closer study it may be cleared up. In context, when Paul uses the term "Christ" in Romans 10:6-7, he means "the system of doctrine taught by Christ." Paul uses the same type of terminology when he talks of "preaching Christ" in Philippians 1:15.) Paul is in the Romans passage demonstrating that it is not beyond the reach of Gentiles to be saved from sin. He proves this by referring to the passage in Deuteronomy where Moses assures the Israelites that it is not beyond their reach to be saved from sin and death. This passage only makes sense if the Christians (both Jews and Gentiles) are regarded by Paul as true members of Israel. Otherwise, Paul seems to be guilty of gross distortion of Scripture.

****

QUOTE #3: (Deut. 31:6 / Heb. 13:5)

Deuteronomy 31:1-6
¹Then Moses went out and spoke these words to all Israel: ²"I am now a hundred and twenty years old and I am no longer able to lead you. The Lord has said to me, 'You shall not cross the Jordan.' ³The Lord your God himself will cross over ahead of you. He will destroy these nations before you, and you will take possession of their land. Joshua also will cross over ahead of you, as the Lord said. ⁴And the Lord will do to them what he did to Sihon and Og, the kings of the Amorites, whom he destroyed along with their land. ⁵The Lord will deliver them to you, and you must do to them all that I have commanded you. ⁶Be strong and courageous. Do not be afraid or terrified because of them, for the Lord your God goes with you; **he will never leave you nor forsake you.**"

Hebrews 13:5-6
⁵Keep your lives free from the love of money and be content with what you have, because God has said, **"Never will I leave you; never will I forsake you."** ⁶So we say with confidence, "The Lord is my helper; I will not be afraid. What can man do to me?"

The author of Hebrews tells the Christians to avoid discontent by realizing that God will never leave or forsake them. But where does he get this comforting statement? From the book of Deuteronomy, where Moses tells the Israelites that God will never leave or forsake the Israelites! Therefore, for the New Testament to make sense, we must suppose that to the author of Hebrews, the Christians were true Israelites. By the way, someone might say, "But the Deuteronomy verses state that God would never leave or forsake the Israelites, so how do you explain your idea that God actually did forsake 'Racial Israel' and replace it with the Church?" To which we would reply with a Scripture passage from the same chapter as our comforting Deuteronomy verse, namely, Deuteronomy 31:16-17: "And the Lord said to Moses: 'You are going to rest with your fathers, and these people will soon prostitute themselves to the foreign gods of the land they are entering. They will forsake me and break the covenant I make with them. On that day I will become angry with them **and forsake them;** I will hide my face from them, and they will be destroyed.'" So, unless we say that God contradicts himself, we must come to the conclusion that the promise of God to "never forsake" Israel was (from the very beginning) conditional upon Israel's obedience to God. And so it is with Christians. As long as we obey God, we may be assured that God is always with us.

QUOTE #4: (Deut. 32:36 / Psa. 135:14 / Heb. 10:30)

Deuteronomy 32:36-38
[36]**The Lord will judge his people** and have compassion on his servants when he sees their strength is gone and no one is left, slave or free. [37]He will say: "Now where are the gods, the rock they took refuge in, [38]the gods who ate the fat of their sacrifices and drank the wine of their drink offerings? Let them rise up to help you! Let them give you shelter!

Psalm 135:8-14
[8]He struck down the firstborn of Egypt, the firstborn of men and animals. [9]He sent his signs and wonders into your midst, O Egypt, against Pharoah and all his servants. [10]He struck down many nations and killed mighty kings-- [11]Sihon king of the Amorites, Og king of Bashan and all the kings of Canaan-- [12]and he gave their land as an inheritance, an inheritance to his people Israel. [13]Your name, O Lord, endures forever, your renown, O Lord, through all generations. [14]For **the Lord will judge his people** and have compassion on his servants.

Hebrews 10:28-31
[28]Anyone who rejected the law of Moses died without mercy on the testimony of two or three witnesses. [29]How much more severely do you think a man deserves to be punished who has trampled the Son of God under foot, who

has treated as an unholy thing the blood of the covenant that sanctified him, and who has insulted the Spirit of grace? [30]For we know him who said, "It is mine to avenge; I will repay," and again, "**The Lord will judge his people**." [31]It is a dreadful thing to fall into the hands of the living God.

****

Deuteronomy and the Psalms both assure the Israelites that God will judge "his people" the Israelites. Hebrews warns the Christians that God will judge "his people" the Christians!

****

QUOTE #5: (Psa. 22:22 / Heb. 2:12)

Psalm 22:22-24
[22]**I will declare your name to my brothers; in the congregation I will praise you.** [23]You who fear the Lord, praise him! All you descendants of Jacob, honor him! Revere him, all you descendants of Israel! [24]For he has not despised or disdained the suffering of the afflicted one; he has not hidden his face from him but has listened to his cry for help.

Hebrews 2:9-15
[9]But we see Jesus, who was made a little lower than the angels, now crowned with glory and honor because he suffered death, so that by the grace of God he might taste death for everyone. [10]In bringing many sons to glory, it was fitting that God, for whom and through whom everything exists, should make the author of their salvation perfect through suffering. [11]Both the one who makes men holy and those who are made holy are of the same family. So Jesus is not ashamed to call them brothers. [12]He says, "**I will declare your name to my brothers; in the presence of the congregation I will sing your praises.**" [13]And again, "I will put my trust in him." And again he says, "Here am I, and the children God has given me." [14]Since the children have flesh and blood, he too shared in their humanity so that by his death he might destroy him who holds the power of death--that is, the devil-- [15]and free those who all their lives were held in slavery by their fear of death.

****

In Psalm 22, the Christ is prophesied to "declare God's name to his brothers" who are Israelites. Yet the author of Hebrews says that the Christ's brothers are "those who are made holy" (Hebrews 2:11), that is, Christians! Once again, unless we concede that the quote in Hebrews is woefully out of context, we must conclude that the Church is Israel according to the New Testament.

****

QUOTE #6: (Psa. 44:22 / Rom. 8:36)

Psalm 44:4-11, 22
⁴'You are my King and my God, who decrees victories for Jacob. ⁵Through you we push back our enemies; through your name we trample our foes. ⁶I do not trust in my bow, my sword does not bring me victory; ⁷but you give us victory over our enemies, you put our adversaries to shame. ⁸In God we make our boast all day long, and we will praise your name forever. Selah ⁹But now you have rejected and humbled us; you no longer go out with our armies. ¹⁰You made us retreat before the enemy, and our adversaries have plundered us. ¹¹You gave us up to be devoured like sheep and have scattered us among the nations. . . . ²²**Yet for your sake we face death all day long; we are considered as sheep to be slaughtered.**

Romans 8:35-39
³⁵Who shall separate us from the love of Christ? Shall trouble or hardship or persecution or famine or nakedness or danger or sword? ³⁶As it is written: **"For your sake we face death all day long; we are considered as sheep to be slaughtered."** ³⁷No, in all these things we are more than conquerers through him who loved us. ³⁸For I am convinced that neither death nor life, neither angels nor demons, neither the present nor the future, nor any powers, ³⁹neither height nor depth, nor anything else in all creation, will be able to separate us from the love of God that is in Christ Jesus our Lord.

****
Paul quotes a verse which talks about the persecution of Israelites and refers it to Christians undergoing tribulations.

****

QUOTE #7: (Psa. 95:7-11 / Heb. 3:7-11)

Psalm 95:6-11
⁶Come, let us bow down in worship, let us kneel before the Lord our Maker; ⁷for he is our God and we are the people of his pasture, the flock under his care. **Today, if you hear his voice, ⁸do not harden your hearts as you did at Meribah, as you did that day at Massah in the desert, ⁹where your fathers tested and tried me, though they had seen what I did. ¹⁰For forty years I was angry with that generation; I said, "They are a people whose hearts go astray, and they have not known my ways." ¹¹So I declared on oath in my anger, "They shall never enter my rest."**

Hebrews 3:7-19

[7]So, as the Holy Spirit says: **"Today, if you hear his voice, [8]do not harden your hearts as you did in the rebellion, during the time of testing in the desert, [9]where your fathers tested and tried me and for forty years saw what I did. [10]That is why I was angry with that generation, and I said, 'Their hearts are always going astray, and they have not known my ways.' [11]So I declared on oath in my anger, 'They shall never enter my rest.' "** [12]See to it, brothers, that none of you has a sinful, unbelieving heart that turns away from the living God. [13]But encourage one another daily, as long as it is called Today, so that none of you may be hardened by sin's deceitfulness. [14]We have come to share in Christ if we hold firmly till the end the confidence we had at first. [15]As has just been said: "Today, if you hear his voice, do not harden your hearts as you did in the rebellion." [16]Who were they who heard and rebelled? Were they not all those who Moses led out of Egypt? [7]And with whom was he angry for forty years? Was it not with those who sinned, whose bodies fell in the desert? [18]And to whom did God swear that they would never enter his rest if not to those who disobeyed? [19]So we see that they were not able to enter, because of their unbelief.

QUOTE #8: (Psa. 130:8/Tit. 2:14)

Psalm 130:7-8

[7]O Israel, put your hope in the Lord, for with the Lord is unfailing love and with him is full redemption. **[8]He himself will redeem Israel from all their sins.**

Titus 2:11-14

[11]For the grace of God that brings salvation has appeared to all men. [12]It teaches us to say "No" to ungodliness and worldly passions, and to live self-controlled, upright and godly lives in this present age, [13]while we wait for the blessed hope--the glorious appearing of our great God and Savior, Jesus Christ, [14]who **gave himself for us to redeem us from all wickedness** and to purify for himself a people that are his very own, eager to do what is good.

QUOTE #9: (Isa. 28:16 / Rom. 10:11 / Eph. 2:20 / 1 Pet. 2:6)

Isaiah 28:14-16

[14]Therefore hear the word of the Lord, you scoffers who rule this people in Jerusalem. [15]You boast, "We have entered into a covenant with death, with the grave we have made an agreement. When an overwhelming scourge sweeps by, it cannot touch us, for we have made a lie our refuge and falsehood our hiding place." [16]So this is what the Sovereign Lord says: **"See, I lay a stone in Zion, a tested stone, a precious cornerstone for a sure foundation; the one who trusts will never be dismayed."**

Note that this verse says that the "stone", the "tested stone", the "chief cornerstone" (that is, the Messiah) will be a sure foundation IN ZION. The New Testament is quite fond of this verse, using it at least three times in the following passages. However, instead of locating the fulfillment of the passage in Palestine, the fulfillment is seen to be in the entire world among Christians of Jewish and Gentile origin. How is this possible unless Zion is now devoid of all geographical connotations, and refers to the Church?

Romans 10:9-13
⁹That if you confess with your mouth, "Jesus is Lord," and believe in your heart that God raised him from the dead, you will be saved. ¹⁰For it is with your heart that you believe and are justified, and it is with your mouth that you confess and are saved. ¹¹As the Scripture says, "**Anyone who trusts in him will never be put to shame.**" ¹²For there is no difference between Jew and Gentile--the same Lord is Lord of all and richly blesses all who call on him, ¹³for, "Everyone who calls on the name of the Lord will be saved."

Ephesians 2:19-22
¹⁹Consequently, you are no longer foreigners and aliens, but fellow citizens with God's people and members of God's household, ²⁰built on **the foundation** of the apostles and prophets, with Christ Jesus himself **as the chief cornerstone.** ²¹In him the whole building is joined together and rises to become a holy temple in the Lord. ²²And in him you too are being built together to become a dwelling in which God lives by his Spirit.

1 Peter 2:4-8
⁴As you come to him, the living Stone--rejected by men but chosen by God and precious to him-- ⁵you also, like living stones, are being built into a spiritual house to be a holy priesthood, offering spiritual sacrifices acceptable to God through Jesus Christ. ⁶For in Scripture it says: "**See, I lay a stone in Zion, a chosen and precious cornerstone, and the one who trusts in him will never be put to shame.**" ⁷Now to you who believe, this stone is precious. But to those who do not believe, "The stone the builders rejected has become the capstone," ⁸and, "A stone that causes men to stumble and a rock that makes them fall." They stumble because they disobey the message--which is also what they were destined for.

QUOTE #10: (Isa. 49:8 / 2 Cor. 6:2)

Isaiah 49:1-21
¹Listen to me, you islands; hear this, you distant nations: Before I was born the Lord called me; from my birth he has made mention of my name. ²He made my mouth like a sharpened sword, in the shadow of his hand he hid me; he made me into a polished arrow and concealed me in his quiver. ³He said to

me, "You are my servant, Israel, in whom I will display my splendor." ⁴But I said, "I have labored to no purpose; I have spent my strength in vain and for nothing. Yet what is due me is in the Lord's hand, and my reward is with my God." ⁵And now the Lord says--he who formed me in the womb to be his servant to bring Jacob back to him and gather Israel to himself, for I am honored in the eyes of the Lord and my God has been my strength-- ⁶he says: "It is too small a thing for you to be my servant to restore the tribes of Jacob and bring back those of Israel I have kept. I will also make you a light for the Gentiles, that you may bring my salvation to the ends of the earth," ⁷This is what the Lord says--the Redeemer and Holy One of Israel--to him who was despised and abhorred by the nation, to the servant of rulers: "Kings will see you and rise up, princes will see and bow down, because of the Lord, who is faithful, the Holy One of Israel, who has chosen you." ⁸This is what the Lord says: **"In the time of my favor I will answer you, and in the day of salvation I will help you**; I will keep you and will make you to be a covenant for the people, to restore the land and to reassign its desolate inheritances, ⁹to say to the captives, 'Come out,' and to those in darkness, 'Be free!' "They will feed beside the roads and find pasture on every barren hill. ¹⁰They will neither hunger nor thirst, nor will the desert heat or the sun beat upon them. He who has compassion on them will guide them and lead them beside springs of water. ¹¹I will turn all my mountains into roads, and my highways will be raised up. ¹²See, they will come from afar--some from the north, some from the west, some from the region of Aswan." ¹³Shout for joy, O heavens; rejoice, O earth; burst into song, O mountains! For the Lord comforts his people and will have compassion on his afflicted ones. ¹⁴But Zion said, "The Lord has forsaken me, the Lord has forgotten me." ¹⁵"Can a mother forget the baby at her breast and have no compassion on the child she has borne? Though she may forget, I will not forget you! ¹⁶See, I have engraved you on the palms of my hands; your walls are ever before me. ¹⁷Your sons hasten back, and those who laid you waste depart from you. ¹⁸Lift up your eyes and look around; all your sons gather and come to you. As surely as I live," declares the Lord, "you will wear them all as ornaments; you will put them on, like a bride. ¹⁹"Though you were ruined and made desolate and your land laid waste, now you will be too small for your people, and those who devoured you will be far away. ²⁰The children born during your bereavement will yet say in your hearing, 'This place is too small for us; give us more space to live in.' ²¹Then you will say in your heart, 'Who bore me these? I was bereaved and barren; I was exiled and rejected. Who brought these up? I was left all alone, but these--where have they come from?' "

2 Corinthians 6:1-2
¹As God's fellow workers we urge you not to receive God's grace in vain. ²For he says, **"In the time of my favor I heard you, and in the day of salvation I helped you."** I tell you, now is the time of God's favor, now is the day of salvation.

In 2 Corinthians, Paul quotes Isaiah 49:8 to tell the Corinthians that right now is the proper time to be concerned about salvation. The interesting thing about this quote is that Isaiah 49 is about the coming of the Christ, and in Isaiah 49:8, God promises to answer the requests of the Christ and help him in the "day of salvation." In the same verse, God also promises to "restore the land" of Israel and "reassign its desolate inheritances." Verses after 49:8 talk about the regathering of the Israelites to the desolation of Israel, which then prospers and is comforted by God. Now, is this what happened in the times of Christ and the Apostles? No, it is not. The literal land of Israel was devastated during two massive wars, and finally the Jews were expelled from Jerusalem altogether. How is it possible, then, for Paul to say that Isaiah 49 referred to the times in which he lived? Because when the passage is taken away from 'Racial Israel' and given to the Israel of God, it is talking about the building up of Spiritual Zion, the Church. It is talking about repairing the desolate spots of the world by conversion to Christ. Wherever a conversion to Christ takes place, there a "captive" is set free, as Isaiah 49:9 says.

QUOTE #11: (Isa. 52:7 / Rom. 10:15)

Isaiah 52:1-10
[1]Awake, awake, O Zion, clothe yourself with strength. Put on your garments of splendor, O Jerusalem, the holy city. The uncircumcised and defiled will not enter you again. [2]Shake off your dust; rise up, sit enthroned, O Jerusalem. Free yourself from the chains on your neck, O captive Daughter of Zion. [3]For this is what the Lord says: "You were sold for nothing, and without money you will be redeemed." [4]For this is what the Sovereign Lord says: "At first my people went down to Egypt to live; lately, Assyria has opposed them. [5]"And now what do I have here?" declares the Lord. "For my people have been taken away for nothing, and those who rule them mock," declares the Lord. "And all day long my name is constantly blasphemed. [6] Therefore my people will know my name; therefore in that day they will know that it is I who foretold it. Yes, it is I." [7]**How beautiful on the mountains are the feet of those who bring good news,** who proclaim peace, who bring good tidings, who proclaim salvation, who say to Zion, "Your God reigns!" [8]Listen! Your watchmen lift up their voices; together they shout for joy. When the Lord returns to Zion, they will see it with their own eyes. [9]Burst into songs of joy together, you ruins of Jerusalem, for the Lord has comforted his people, he has redeemed Jerusalem. [10]The Lord will lay bare his holy arm in the sight of all the nations, and all the ends of the earth will see the salvation of our God.

58

Romans 10:13-15

[13]for, "Everyone who calls on the name of the Lord will be saved." [14]How, then, can they call on the one they have not believed in? And how can they believe in the one of whom they have not heard? And how can they hear without someone preaching to them? [15]And how can they preach unless they are sent? As it is written, **"How beautiful are the feet of those who bring good news!"**

****

Isaiah the prophet prophesies a time when the "good news" (the gospel) will be proclaimed to Jerusalem (52:7). But let us look at this "good news" more closely. In Isaiah 52:1, we are told that the uncircumcised will not enter into Zion. In 52:2, we see that the enslaved Israelites will be freed. The Lord will return to Zion (52:8), and the ruins of Jerusalem will be rebuilt. All this may be seen by reading our Old Testament selection. But Paul quotes 52:7 and refers it to those who spread the "good news" about Jesus the Christ. In Isaiah, the messengers go to desolate Jerusalem, and in the New Testament, the messengers go into the world of sinners, resulting in conversion! Once again, Paul has stripped the Isaiah passage of its geography and its race-consciousness, and referred it to the New Israel, the Christian Church. Further, it is the spiritually uncircumcised who are not allowed into the Church of God, and the physical member no longer has anything to do with entering into Jerusalem.

****

QUOTE #12: (Isa. 54:1 / Gal. 4:27)

Isaiah 54:1-8

[1]**"Sing, O barren woman, you who never bore a child; burst into song, shout for joy, you who were never in labor; because more are the children of the desolate woman than of her who has a husband," says the Lord.** [2]"Enlarge the place of your tent, stretch your tent curtains wide, do not hold back; lengthen your cords, strengthen your stakes. [3] For you will spread out to the right and to the left; your descendants will dispossess nations and settle in their desolate cities. [4]"Do not be afraid; you will not suffer shame. Do not fear disgrace; you will not be humiliated. You will forget the shame of your youth and remember no more the reproach of your widowhood. [5]For your Maker is your husband--the Lord Almighty is his name--the Holy One of Israel is your redeemer; he is called the God of all the earth. [6]The Lord will call you back as if you were a wife deserted and distressed in spirit--a wife who married young, only to rejected," says your God. [7]"For a brief moment I abandoned you, but with deep compassion I will bring you back. [8]In a surge of anger I hid my face from you for a moment, but with everlasting kindness I will have compassion on you," says the Lord your Redeemer.

Galatians 4:21-31

²¹Tell me, you who want to be under the law, are you not aware of what the law says? ²²For it is written that Abraham had two sons, one by the slave woman and the other by the free woman. ²³His son by the slave woman was born in the ordinary way; but his son by the free woman was born as the result of a promise. ²⁴These things may be taken figuratively, for the women represent two covenants. One covenant is from Mount Sinai and bears children who are to be slaves: This is Hagar. ²⁵Now Hagar stands for Mount Sinai in Arabia and corresponds to the present city of Jerusalem, because she is in slavery with her children. ²⁶But the Jerusalem that is above is free, and she is our mother. ²⁷For it is written: **"Be glad, O barren woman, who bears no children; break forth and cry aloud, you who have no labor pains; because more are the children of the desolate woman than of her who has a husband."** ²⁸Now you, brothers, like Isaac, are children of promise. ²⁹At that time the son born in the ordinary way persecuted the son born by the power of the Spirit. It is the same now. ³⁰But what does the Scripture say? "Get rid of the slave woman and her son, for the slave woman's son will never share in the inheritance with the free woman's son." ³¹Therefore, brothers, we are not children of the slave woman, but of the free woman.

****

Isaiah prophesies a time when Zion will greatly expand, and will conquer foreign nations (54:1-2). Paul says that the passage refers to the Heavenly Zion (the Christian Church) which is having many children. Once again, a passage in the Old Testament has been taken from "Racial Israel" (because of sin, as we learn from other passages) and applied to Christians.

****

QUOTE #13: (Jer. 31:31-34 / Heb. 8:8-12)

Jeremiah 31:31-35

³¹**"The time is coming," declares the Lord," when I will make a new covenant with the house of Israel and with the house of Judah. ³²It will not be like the covenant I made with their forefathers when I took them by the hand to lead them out of Egypt, because they broke my covenant, though I was a husband to them," declares the Lord. ³³"This is the covenant I will make with the house of Israel after that time," declares the Lord. "I will put my law in their minds and write it in their hearts. I will be their God, and they will be my people. ³⁴No longer will a man teach his neighbor, or a man his brother, saying, 'Know the Lord,' because they will all know me, from the least of them to the greatest," declares the Lord. "For I will forgive their wickedness and will remember their sins no more."** ³⁵This is what the Lord says, he who appoints the sun to shine by day, who decrees the moon and stars to shine by night, who stirs up the sea so that its waves roar--the Lord Almighty is his name.

Hebrews 8:6-13

⁶But the ministry Jesus has received is as superior to theirs as the covenant of which he is mediator is superior to the old one, and it is founded on better promises. ⁷For if there had been nothing wrong with that first covenant, no place would have been sought for another. ⁸But God found fault with the people and said: "**The time is coming, declares the Lord, when I will make a new covenant with the house of Israel and with the house of Judah. ⁹It will not be like the covenant I made with their forefathers when I took them by the hand to lead them out of Egypt, because they did not remain faithful to my covenant, and I turned away from them, declares the Lord. ¹⁰This is the covenant I will make with the house of Israel after that time, declares the Lord. I will put my laws in their minds and write them on their hearts. I will be their God, and they will be my people. ¹¹No longer will a man teach his neighbor, or a man his brother, saying, 'Know the Lord,' because they will all know me, from the least of them to the greatest. ¹²For I will forgive their wickedness and will remember their sins no more.**" ¹³By calling this covenant "new", he has made the first one obsolete; and what is obsolete and aging will soon disappear.

****

Jeremiah the prophet says that the Mosaic Covenant will be discarded in his future because of continued Israelite disobedience to God (31:32). In place of this covenant God will make a "new covenant" (31:31). And with whom does God make this covenant? With "the house of Israel and the house of Judah"! Even the New Testament quotes that part of the prophecy, and yet refers the prophecy to the Christians! Again, how is this possible, unless the author of Hebrews viewed the Christians as the true Israel?

****

QUOTE #14: (Hos. 1:10 & 2:23 / Rom. 9:25-26 / 1 Pet. 2:10)

Hosea 1:1-11

¹The word of the Lord that came to Hosea son of Beeri during the reigns of Uzziah, Jotham, Ahaz and Hezekiah, kings of Judah, and during the reign of Jeroboam son of Jehoash king of Israel: ²When the Lord began to speak through Hosea, the Lord said to him, "Go, take to yourself an adulterous wife and children of unfaithfulness, because the land is guilty of the vilest adultery in departing from the Lord." ³So he married Gomer daughter of Diblaim, and she conceived and bore him a son. ⁴Then the Lord said to Hosea, "Call him Jezreel, because I will soon punish the house of Jehu for the massacre at Jezreel, and I will put an end to the kingdom of Israel. ⁵In that day I will break Israel's bow in the Valley of Jezreel." ⁶Gomer conceived again and gave birth to a daughter. Then the Lord said to Hosea, "Call her Lo-Ruhamah, for I will no longer show love to the house of Israel, that I

should at all forgive them. ⁷Yet I will show love to the house of Judah; and I will save them--not by bow, sword or battle, or by horses and horsemen, but by the Lord their God." ⁸After she had weaned Lo-Ruhamah, Gomer had another son. ⁹Then the Lord said, "Call him Lo-Ammi, for you are not my people, and I am not your God. ¹⁰"Yet the Israelites will be like the sand on the seashore, which cannot be measured or counted. **In the place where it was said to them, 'You are not my people,' they will be called 'sons of the living God.'** ¹¹The people of Judah and the people of Israel will be reunited, and they will appoint one leader and will come up out of the land, for great will be the day of Jezreel.

Hosea 2:21-23
²¹"In that day I will respond," declares the Lord--"I will respond to the skies, and they will respond to the earth; ²²and the earth will respond to the grain, the new wine and oil, and they will respond to Jezreel. ²³I will plant her for myself in the land; I will show my love to the one I called 'Not my loved one.' **I will say to those called 'Not my people,' 'You are my people';** and they will say, 'You are my God.'"

Romans 9:22-26
²²What if God, choosing to show his wrath and make his power known, bore with great patience the objects of his wrath--prepared for destruction? ²³What if he did this to make the riches of his glory known to the object of his mercy, whom he prepared in advance for glory-- ²⁴even us, whom he also called, not only from the Jews but also from the Gentiles? ²⁵As he says in Hosea: **"I will call them 'my people' who are not my people;** and I will call her 'my loved one' who is not my loved one," ²⁶and, **"It will happen that in the very place where it was said to them, 'You are not my people,' they will be called 'sons of the living God.'"**

1 Peter 2:9-10
⁹But you are a chosen people, a royal priesthood, a holy nation, a people belonging to God, that you may declare the praises of him who called you out of darkness into his wonderful light. ¹⁰**Once you were not a people, but now you are the people of God;** once you had not received mercy, but now you have received mercy.

****

In Hosea, God announces that the people of Israel, due to sin, are not the people of God any longer. However, God hasn't finished with Israel yet, and prophesies a time in the future in which the Israelites will again be called people of God (1:10, 2:23). Paul and Peter both quote the Hosea passages as referring to Gentiles who became converts to Christ, a position which is impossible to hold unless the privileges of Israel now apply to anyone, regardless of physical descent, so long as he or she is willing to repent and obey God's word. So, the Church is the real Israel now.

****

QUOTE #15: (Hos. 13:14 / 1 Cor. 15:55)

Hosea 13:9-16

[9]"You are destroyed, O Israel, because you are against me, against your helper. [10]Where is your king, that he may save you? Where are your rulers in all your towns, of whom you said, 'Give me a king and princes'? [11]So in my anger I gave you a king, and in my wrath I took him away. [12]The guilt of Ephraim is stored up, his sins are kept on record. [13]Pains as of a woman in childbirth come to him, but he is a child without wisdom; when the time arrives, he does not come to the opening of the womb. [14]"I will ransom them from the power of the grave; I will redeem them from death. **Where, O death, are your plagues? Where, O grave, is your destruction?** "I will have no compassion, [15]even though he thrives among his brothers. An east wind from the Lord will come, blowing in from the desert; his spring will fail and his well dry up. His storehouse will be plundered of all its treasures. [16]The people of Samaria must bear their guilt, because they have rebelled against their God. They will fall by the sword; their little ones will be dashed to the ground, their pregnant women ripped open."

1 Corinthians 15:50-55

[50]I declare to you, brothers, that flesh and blood cannot inherit the kingdom of God, nor does the perishable inherit the imperishable. [51]Listen, I tell you a mystery: We will not all sleep, but we will all be changed-- [52]in a flash, in the twinkling of an eye, at the last trumpet. For the trumpet will sound, the dead will be raised imperishable, and we will be changed. [53]For the perishable must clothe itself with the imperishable, and the mortal with immortality. [54]When the perishable has been clothed with the imperishable, and the mortal with immortality, then the saying that is written will come true: "Death has been swallowed up in victory." [55]**"Where, O death, is your victory? Where, O death, is your sting?"**

****

Many people quote Paul's passage on the resurrection, "Where, O death, is your victory? Where, O death is your sting?", without realizing where this saying comes from. Its origin is in Hosea 13:14, where it refers to God resurrecting Israelites from the grave, the land of the dead. However, in 1 Corinthians, Paul uses it to prove the resurrection of those who inherit the kingdom of God, that is, the believers in Christ. It is not possible to get this proof out of Hosea 13:14, unless we presuppose that the Christian Church is now the Israel of God.

****

QUOTE #16: (Joel 2:32 / Rom. 10:13)

Joel 2:32
[32]And **everyone who calls on the name of the Lord will be saved;** for on Mount Zion and in Jerusalem there will deliverance, as the Lord has said, among the survivors whom the Lord calls.

Romans 10:9-13
[9]That if you confess with your mouth, "Jesus is Lord," and believe in your heart that God raised him from the dead, you will be saved. [10]For it is with your heart that you believe and are justified, and it is with your mouth that you confess and are saved. [11]As the Scripture says, "Anyone who trusts in him will never be put to shame." [12]For there is no difference between Jew and Gentile--the same Lord is Lord of all and richly blesses all who call on him, [13]for, **"Everyone who calls on the name of the Lord will be saved."**

****

Joel the prophet says that "everyone who calls on the name of the Lord will be saved." A lot of people know this phrase, but know it only from Romans 10:13. Notably, Joel gives the location of where people will call upon the Lord: "on Mount Zion and in Jerusalem," places which are quite remote from Rome, where the people Paul was writing to lived. Paul makes no sense applying this passage to Christians, unless (once again!) this passage has been taken from "Racial Israel" and now belongs to true Israel, that is, the Church.

****

SECTION 3

Old Testament Ethical Commands To Israel Which Are Quoted In The New Testament As Applying To The Church

The quotes themselves are in bold type to call the reader's attention to them. The surrounding (non-bold) verses are included so that the context may be examined.

These verses demonstrate that the New Testament regards the Church as Israel, because of the fact that Old Testament ethical commands to Israel are repeatedly quoted as referring to Christian rules of conduct.

QUOTE #1: (Exo. 16:18 / 2 Cor. 8:15)

Exodus 16:13-18

¹³That evening quail came and covered the camp, and in the morning there was a layer of dew around the camp. ¹⁴When the dew was gone, thin flakes like frost on the ground appeared on the desert floor. ¹⁵When the Israelites saw it, they said to each other, "What is it?" For they did not know what it was. Moses said to them, "It is the bread the Lord has given you to eat. ¹⁶This is what the Lord has commanded: "Each one is to gather as much as he needs. Take an omer for each person you have in your tent.'" ¹⁷The Israelites did as they were told; some gathered much, some little. ¹⁸And when they measured it by the omer, **he who gathered much did not have too much, and he who gathered little did not have too little.** Each one gathered as much as he needed.

2 Corinthians 8:13-15

¹³Our desire is not that others might be relieved while you are hard pressed, but that there might be equality. ¹⁴At the present time your plenty will supply what they need, so that in turn their plenty will supply what you need. Then there will be equality, ¹⁵as it is written: **"He who gathered much did not have too much, and he who gathered little did not have too little."**

****

What is stated as a fact regarding the gathering of manna by Israel is regarded as a standard for Christian charity by the apostle Paul (!), and with not one word of explanation as to how this can be. How can Paul figure on the Corinthians accepting his exegesis, unless both he and they suppose the Christian Church to be the Israel of the New Testament?

****

QUOTE #2: (Lev. 11:45 / 19:2 / 1 Pet. 1:16)

Leviticus 11:44-45

⁴⁴I am the Lord your God; consecrate yourselves and be holy, because I am holy. Do not make yourselves unclean by any creature that moves about on the ground. ⁴⁵I am the Lord who brought you up out of Egypt to be your God; therefore **be holy, because I am holy.**

Leviticus 19:1-3

¹The Lord said to Moses, ²"Speak to the entire assembly of Israel and say to them: '**Be holy because I, the Lord your God, am holy.** ³" 'Each of you must respect his mother and father, and you must observe my Sabbaths. I am the Lord your God.

1 Peter 1:13-16

[13]Therefore, prepare your minds for action; be self-controlled; set your hope fully on the grace to be given you when Jesus Christ is revealed. [14]As obedient children, do not conform to the evil desires you had when you lived in ignorance. [15]But just as he who called you is holy, so be holy in all you do; [16]for it is written: **Be holy, because I am holy."**

****

Peter instructs Christians to be holy in all actions, because of God stating to Israelites in Leviticus: "Be holy, because I am holy." Look at the sources for this declaration by God, and you will notice a surprising (or, perhaps, not so surprising!) circumstance. Namely, this declaration by God was used in order to instruct the Israelites about the seriousness of abstaining from unclean foods. In our second Leviticus passage, God says: "Be holy. . ." at least partially in regard to sabbath keeping, a command of God which is now abrogated (Colossians 2:16, at least in regard to the day of the week). We can see that, although the particular ceremonial rules of conduct have changed, the idea that Israel must be holy, because God is holy, is constant, Old or New Testament.

****

QUOTE #3: (Deut. 5:16 / Eph. 6:2-3)

Deuteronomy 5:16
[16]**"Honor your father and your mother,** as the Lord your God has commanded you, **so that you may live long and that it may go well with you in the land the Lord your God is giving you.**

Ephesians 6:1-3
[1]Children, obey your parents in the Lord, for this is right. [2]**"Honor your father and mother"**--which is the first commandment with a promise--[3]**"that it may go well with you and that you may enjoy long life on the earth."**

****

Paul quotes the commandment on honoring father and mother, and then the blessing of the commandment, from Deuteronomy. In Ephesians, however, the blessing is somewhat changed from the original. While in Deuteronomy God promises a long life in "the land of the Lord your God is giving you," that is, in the land of Israel, Paul says that God promises a long life to anyone anywhere "on the earth," an interesting fact in that the Church is non-geographical, as John 4:19-24 states. So the moral command of Deuteronomy is retained, but without the geographical qualifications!

****

QUOTE #4: (Deut. 17:7 / 19:19 / 22:24 / 24:7 / 1 Cor. 5:13)

Deuteronomy 17:2-7

²If a man or woman living among you in one of the towns the Lord gives you is found doing evil in the eyes of the Lord your God in violation of his covenant, ³and contrary to my command has worshiped other gods, bowing down to them or to the sun or the moon or the stars of the sky, ⁴and this has been brought to your attention, then you must investigate it thoroughly. If it is true and it has been proved that this detestable thing has been done in Israel, ⁵take the man or woman who has done this evil deed to your city gate and stone that person to death. ⁶On the testimony of two or three witnesses a man shall be put to death, but no one shall be put to death on the testimony of only one witness. ⁷The hands of the witnesses must be the first in putting him to death, and then the hands of all the people. **You must purge the evil from among you.**

Deuteronomy 19:19

¹⁹then do to him as he intended to do to his brother. **You must purge the evil from among you.**

Deuteronomy 22:24

²⁴you shall take both of them to the gate of that town and stone them to death--the girl because she was in the town and did not scream for help, and the man because he violated another man's wife. **You must purge the evil from among you.**

Deuteronomy 24:7

⁷If a man is caught kidnapping one of his brother Israelites and treats him as a slave or sells him, the kidnapper must die. **You must purge the evil from among you.**

1 Corinthians 5:9-13

⁹I have written you in my letter not to associate with sexually immoral people-- ¹⁰not at all meaning the people of this world who are immoral, or the greedy and swindlers, or idolators. In that case you would have to leave this world. ¹¹But now I am writing you that you must not associate with anyone who calls himself a brother but is sexually immoral or greedy, an idolator or a slanderer, a drunkard or a swindler. With such a man do not even eat. ¹²What business is it of mine to judge those outside the church? Are you not to judge those inside? ¹³God will judge those outside. **"Expel the wicked man from among you."**

****

Paul quotes from an oft-repeated verse in Deuteronomy: "Expel the wicked man from among you," and, without a word of explanation, says to the Christians of the city of Corinth (a Gentile city) that this principle of Israel applies to them.

****

QUOTE #5: (Deut. 19:15 / 2 Cor. 13:1 / 1 Tim. 5:19)

Deuteronomy 19:11-15
¹¹But if a man hates his neighbor and lies in wait for him, assaults and kills him, and then flees to one of those cities, ¹²the elders of his town shall send for him, bring him back from the city, and hand him over to the avenger of blood to die. ¹³Show him no pity. You must purge from Israel the guilt of shedding innocent blood, so that it may go well with you. ¹⁴Do not move your neighbor's boundary stone set up by your predecessors in the inheritance you receive in the land the Lord your God is giving you to possess. ¹⁵One witness is not enough to convict a man accused of any crime or offense he may have committed. **A matter must be established by the testimony of two or three witnesses.**

2 Corinthians 13:1-3
¹This will be my third visit to you. **"Every matter must be established by the testimony of two or three witnesses."** ²I already gave you a warning when I was with you the second time. I now repeat it while absent: On my return I will not spare those who sinned earlier or any of the others, ³since you are demanding proof that Christ is speaking through me. He is not weak in dealing with you, but is powerful among you.

1 Timothy 5:19-20
¹⁹Do not entertain an accusation against an elder **unless it is brought by two or three witnesses.** ²⁰Those who sin are to be rebuked publicly, so that others may take warning.

****

Paul says that all offenses tried in a church court must be validated by two or three witnesses, which coincidentally is the same rule which was in effect in the courts of Old Testament Israel.

****

QUOTE #6: Isa. 35:3 / Heb. 12:12)

Isaiah 35:1-8
¹The desert and the parched land will be glad; the wilderness will rejoice and blossom. Like the crocus, ²it will burst into bloom; it will rejoice greatly and shout for joy. The glory of Lebanon will be given to it, the splendor of Carmel and Sharon; they will see the glory of the Lord, the splendor of our God. ³**Strengthen the feeble hands, steady the knees that give way;** ⁴say to those with fearful hearts, "Be strong, do not fear; your God will come, he will come with vengeance; with divine retribution he will come to save you." ⁵Then will the eyes of the blind be opened and the ears of the deaf unstopped. ⁶Then will the the lame leap like a deer, and the mute tongue shout for joy. Water will gush forth in the wilderness and streams in the desert. ⁷The burning sand will become a pool, the thirsty ground bubbling springs. In the haunts where jackals once lay, grass and reeds and papyrus will grow. ⁸And a highway will be there; it will be called the Way of Holiness. The unclean

will not journey on it; it will be for those who walk in that way; wicked fools will not go about on it.

Hebrews 12:10-13
[10]Our fathers disciplined us for a little while as they thought best; but God disciplines us for our good, that we may share in his holiness. [11]No discipline seems pleasant at the time, but painful. Later on, however. it produces a harvest of righteousness and peace for those who have been trained by it. [12]**Therefore, strengthen your feeble arms and weak knees.** [13]Make level paths for your feet," so that the lame may not be disabled, but rather healed.

****

The author of Hebrews takes a passage which in Isaiah is referring to Israelites on the way to Zion, and refers it to Christians.

****

QUOTE #7: (Isa. 48:20 & 52:11 / 2 Cor. 6:17)

Isaiah 48:20
[20]**Leave Babylon, flee from the Babylonians!** Announce this with shouts of joy and proclaim it. Send it out to the ends of the earth; say, "The Lord has redeemed his servant Jacob."

Isaiah 52:10-12
[10]The Lord will lay bare his holy arm in the sight of all the nations, and all the ends of the earth will see the salvation of our God. [11]**Depart, depart, go out from there! Touch no unclean thing! Come out from it and be pure,** you who carry the vessels of the Lord. [12]But you will not leave in haste or go in flight; for the Lord will go before you, the God of Israel will be your rear guard.

2 Corinthians 6:14-17
[14]Do not be yoked together with unbelievers. For what do righteousness and wickedness have in common? Or what fellowship can light have with darkness? [15]What harmony is there between Christ and Belial? What does a believer have in common with an unbeliever? [16]What agreement is there between the temple of God and idols? For we are the temple of the living God. As God has said: "I will live with them and walk among them, and I will be their God, and they will be my people." [17]**"Therefore come out from them and be separate, says the Lord. Touch no unclean thing,** and I will receive you."

****

The Prophet Isaiah tells the Israelites in Babylon to leave Babylon, touching no unclean thing and taking with them the temple vessels, to restart the worship of God in Jerusalem's temple. Paul says that the passage proves that Gentile converts to Christianity should leave the fellowship and institutions of paganism. Once again, Paul has quoted a verse greatly out of context, unless the Christians are Israel now.

****

INDEX

73

CPSIA information can be obtained
at www.ICGtesting.com
Printed in the USA
FSHW020735020219